Why History Repeats

Mass Movements and the Generations
Past–Present–Future

The Meeting of History with Astrology

Featuring:

Past 2000 Years
History of Christianity
Birth-death of Jesus Christ
Predicting the Future

Theresa H. McDevitt

ISBN: 0-86690-556-1
LCC: 139736, 2-23-04

Second Edition: 2005

Published by:
American Federation of Astrologers, Inc.
6535 S. Rural Road
Tempe, AZ 85283

Printed in the United States of America

I dedicate this book to the memory of my
dear friend Miriam Feierabend, 1907-2003.
She never gave up encouraging me to write.
I regret that she left this world unaware that I was
writing this book. May your soul rest in peace
my celestial sister . . . 'till we meet again.

Special thanks to Anne Sargent and Sioux Rose for their
thoughtful contributions, and to
Darlene Glayat for helping to proofread.
My sincere thanks to all my students for being
a source of inspiration, and to my loving son
and husband for supporting my efforts.

Contents

Foreword

You must be a curious sort if you are reading this page, so this book was written especially for you. It is not just for people who know about astrology, but also for anyone who is wondering how things have happened. It is for someone who wants to understand the patterns and cycles of life, generally and in particular.

It was her interest in astronomy that brought Theresa McDevitt to the study of astrology. "I studied astronomy as a hobby when my children were little," she said. One day in early '70s, she was in a bookstore looking at astronomy books when a book about astrology caught her eye, "and it seemed familiar to me." She said she started reading it, decided to take a correspondence course to learn the math, and in 1983 she took her first exam."

Theresa McDevitt is an unassuming woman with extensive knowledge of world history. She demonstrates that knowledge with her compilation of information about Pluto in this book, and in general discussions about historical events, her recall of the facts is impressive. The specifics she delivers to present her case, that Pluto does influence history on Planet Earth, are quite thought provoking. More than one person has commented to her, "It seems scary that we keep doing the same things over and over again. Why don't we learn?"

McDevitt said she finally decided she needed to find an answer for that question. It is here, in easily readable language, so you can begin to understand the global issues in a new light. You may gain some insight into your own cycles in the process.

There are cycles in life—spring, summer, fall and winter. The moon has phases and circles the earth in 28.5 days. When you begin to study astrology, you must learn the numerical language, which is incontrovertible. But you do not need to know much about astrology, or even believe in it, to discover in this carefully crafted book, how Pluto's transit in the heavens over centuries affects us as individuals and as members of the world community.

Writing in clear, concise sentences of moderate length, McDevitt offers readers a chance to discover how their generation is affected by this major planetary influence. She gives information about the future, which readers can incorporate into their own experience to apply to their own free will.

"I want to make it possible for people to have knowledge that otherwise they would not get because they think astrology is horoscopes in the newspapers. It is not evil to have knowledge. It is not wrong to think. It is important to wake up and look around at what is happening world-wide, and to gain an understanding of how patterns affect us."

Whatever is going on now, Theresa helps us to see that "this too will pass," and perhaps the new knowledge will help everyone to be a participant in positive change.

Anne Sargent

Author's Note: Anne Sargent has been a professional writer and book reviewer for many years. Most recently a writer/editor with the daily St. Augustine Record in Florida, she continues her free-lance writing and reviewing in the Oldest City in America.

Preface

The historical facts presented in this book will help you to discover that not all personal aptitudes derive from the Sun Sign, or inherited genes. Destiny is highly dependent on the particular generational influence of the Plutonian Mass Movement in progress at the time of birth. The cycle of the planet Pluto shows our group karma, or the purpose of our particular generation and the part we must play as individuals. It specifically shows how one generation impacts the next and what to expect when each one begins to stamp its mark upon the world.

History reflects the nature of cycles. Planetary cycles constantly provide the world with a myriad of opportunities by which to learn from history. As mankind learns to avoid the same mistakes it accelerates the evolutionary growth process towards world harmony. Astrological knowledge provides the proven facts and perfect timing, without which, only non-reliable statistics, or merely suppositions based on limited observations exist.

Pluto's cycle promotes plague-like movements that spread through the collective consciousness. Hence, people feel motivated, or compelled to express the issues related to the particular sign being activated by Pluto at the time. Likewise, the generation born absorbs the pertinent qualities of the sign that will identify them as part of a specific group for the rest of their lives.

Astronomy recently declared Pluto to the category of planetoid, due to its relatively small size. Astrology on the other hand, whose observations go beyond physical appearances, has proven Pluto to be a dynamo of influential power upon the world and specifically the generations. Its cycle around the zodiac takes 248.42 years and its erratic orbit causes it to spend from 12 to 33 years in each sign dividing the generations accordingly. Thus, astrologers refer to Pluto as "the generational planet."

Plutonian lessons mainly involve the use, or abuse of power and control. Pluto shows that absolute power corrupts and it leads to self- destruction. Thus, it promotes the rise to power, as well as the fall. Pluto has rulership over the sign Scorpio, which is about death, sex and rebirth, i.e., destruction, regeneration, and transformation. Since its primary purpose is to transform, Pluto begins by exposing to the light the evils that lie within the deepest wells of society. Afterwards, the healing process begins leading to major reforms and significant contributions towards the evolution of humanity.

There is perfect order at work in the universe, if we only take the time to notice. Looking back to previous Mass Movements provides the insight necessary for acquiring a conscious effort to modify the future. Otherwise, destiny will unfold accordingly without significant improvements. The same principles apply to our own personal lives. Awareness of the potentials indicated in our individual birth charts allows us to make improvements in our personal development, thus modifying destiny.

Even though some events are inevitable, or beyond our control, we can still choose how to make the best out of a good, or bad situation. As in the case of weather predictions, awareness of an approaching storm does not give us the power to stop it, but we can take the necessary precautions to avoid the worst. Likewise, cycles come and go hence awareness makes the difference.

The historical compilation presented in this book is relevant to Pluto's influence in its cyclical journey around the zodiac. From the first century A.D. to 2315, the main events that affected the world and will affect it in the future are included herewith. The reader will be able to ascertain that every time Pluto returns to the same sign, the same issues resurface – history repeating itself. Pluto's initial effect is to empower the qualities of the sign thus causing a Mass Movement to occur. After the exuberance, the end result is transmutation and regeneration.

This historical recollection of previous Mass Movements and the obvious effects upon humanity should bring new light to the old slogans; "what goes around, comes around," and "what goes up, must come down." Thus, every new cycle represents a new opportunity for growth and improvements.

Use this book for enlightenment in the studies of life on our magnificent Planet Earth.

Theresa H. McDevitt

Guidelines

1. The primary purpose of this book is to confirm the influence of Pluto's cycle around the zodiac upon world events and the generations.

2. The cycles featured herewith contain enough facts to understand the concept and support the general contention of this book.

3. Every cycle leads to the next and always in accordance to the zodiacal sign. The keywords for each sign and its ruler planet help in the overall assessment of the issues at hand.

4. Within Pluto's cycle there are other planetary influences at work within any given time—they are not addressed in this historical compilation.

5. Towards the end of each cycle, the issues to be dealt with in the cycle that follows are already evident. This information enhances awareness.

6. After Pluto enters a sign, it usually retrogrades to the previous one for a short time. Thus, after the new issues are introduced, there is another opportunity to review the previous ones.

7.People born between two cycles cannot feel they belong to one generation or the other—this is because they are in essence part of both.

8. The consequences of the previous cycle are usually experienced in the cycle that follows.

9. For a better perspective on the trend of events, follow the sequence of the years as they go from past-to-past and fu-

ture-to-future. (Except for the few skipped cycles.)

10. The information presented in this book is strictly based on historical facts, in addition to the amazing relationship between Planet Earth and the "Heavenly Bodies."

11. Highlights:

  a) The Mass Movement (main emphasis, tone, theme, trends, and events at the time (majority of issues relevant to the sign).

  b) The Generation (main thrust, motivation, condition, contributions from those born at the time—past, present, future).

  c) General Impact (effects and consequences of the cycles upon the world and humanity).

12. Knowledge is power—awareness is wisdom.

  a) Know the past, understand the present and be aware of the future. ("Forewarned is Forearmed")

Note: For better comprehension of the sequence of events, this book should be read from the beginning.

Introduction

The world is presently under a Sagittarius Mass Movement (1995-2008). For this reason it makes sense to begin this historical recollection on the Sagittarius Mass Movements, past, present and future. After Sagittarius the rest of the signs will follow in their natural order.

First, it is important to point out that the particular cycle of Pluto in Sagittarius always had a significant effect on America. The influential issues related to the sign Sagittarius and its ruler planet Jupiter, describe the basic fundamental identity of this country:

America is known as "the land of the free" with wide-open spaces and "purple mountains majesty," all nationalities and religions. Strong faith and optimism abide with an emphasis on God, sports, the law, status, travel, adventure, and an insatiable urge for more, bigger, better; plus the fact that it was founded by immigrants; most of whom arrived during the first two Sagittarius cycles after America's discovery. (Refer to the Cycles of Pluto in Sagittarius).

Not surprisingly, the original inhabitants also shared a similar Sagittarius culture: nomadic, free spirited, proud and highly ideological. The symbol of the Sagittarius Centaurs shooting his arrow upwards has spiritual connotations, as well as depicting the image of the brave Native American warriors.

In confirmation to all of the above facts showing the Sagittarius personality, America's birth chart for Independence Day on 7-4-1776 has Sagittarius rising (Ascendant). This is in accordance to the time recorded in Thomas Jefferson's jour-

Inner Wheel
USA
Natal Chart
Jul 4 1776 NS
5:10 pm LMT +5:00:39
Philadelphia, PA
39° N57'08" 075° W09'51"
Geocentric
Tropical
Placidus
True Node

Outer Wheel
Plane/Tower #1
Natal Chart
Sep 11 2001
8:45 pm EDT +4:00
New York, NY
40° N42'51" 074° W00'23"
Geocentric
Tropical
Placidus
True Node

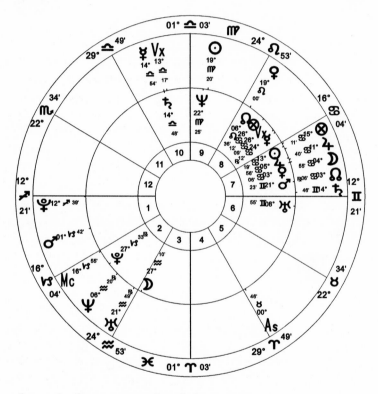

nals, and other congressional documents.

Much historical opinion is in support of Jefferson's account, including the Philadelphia Historical Association, as reported by the classic writings of Manley Palmer Hall in 1941.

The first chart for the USA was calculated and published by English astrologer Ebenezer Sibly in 1787. Sibly was a Free-

xvi

mason and a member of Lodges with intimate trading connections with the USA. He was excellently placed to receive an account of the time the Declaration was signed, from the Freemasons in the USA. They were Washington, Franklin and Hancock, who were mainly responsible for the creation of USA.

The accuracy of Sibly's chart for the Declaration of Independence was confirmed by the resent tragic events of 9-11-2001. At the time, transiting Pluto was at the exact degree of America's Ascendant (12 degrees Sagittarius).

Pluto, the planet of major transformations, conjunct the USA Ascendant (personality) for the first time in American history, forever altered the image and destiny of this Nation. (Refer to previous page for USA chart with planets positions on the outer rim for the event.)

Reinforcing this conjunction was the opposition to Pluto by transiting Saturn. Although the Saturn-Pluto opposition is a cyclic occurrence affecting different zodiacal signs every 31 to 40 years, it had never before impacted the United States directly in this position.

The opposition between these two powerful planets unleashes destructive forces that threaten peace and stability. It heralds a critical period of breakdown and rebuilding, with long lasting consequences.

Although it is beyond human potential to avoid the negative impact of this particular aspect, it is within our power to use this energy as an opportunity to turn the tables on past mistakes, in order to build a better future. On the other hand, destructive forces could use this energy to turn back time, and for abuse of power.

The historical recollection in this book relevant to Pluto's cycle around the zodiac provides further understanding of the present circumstances. Thus, knowing where humanity has been and where it is now, provides the picture of where it is expected to be in the future. This correlation proves that the phrase, "history repeats itself" is not just a supposition—it is a real occurrence.

The art of prediction is directly related to the specific qualities assigned to the 12 astrological signs. Combining this knowledge with the precise science of planetary cycles completes the process.

The purpose of recording history is to learn from it. It provides an excellent venue by which to recognize the undeniable—in order to change destiny. Otherwise, destiny will unfold as usual with limited improvements.

There are 55 cycles of Pluto included in this book pertaining to the past two millenniums and up to the year 2315. These are listed on page xxi.

Before 1201 A.D. some cycles are excluded. Afterwards, the sequences of the years follow a precise order up to 2159.

Synopsis of Main Events Before 1201 A.D.

Pluto was in Virgo in the beginning of the first millennium. By the time Jesus the avatar of the new Pisces Age was killed, Pluto was in Scorpio. During the first century, Jesus' apostles were writing the Gospels. Paul went to Asia Minor and Rome spreading his new version of Judaism – Christendom. Peter and Paul were executed in Rome by Roman authorities. Origen, an Alexandrian theologian put the Old Testament together in six Hebrew and Greek texts (the Hexpla).

Greek mathematician and astronomer, Ptolemy, wrote the first astrological textbook, the Tetrabiblos (still in use today), and drew 26 maps of various countries. The Vikings were invading Europe and Asia.

The first two complete cycles of Pluto around the zodiac from Virgo, back to Virgo twice—from 1 A.D. to 494 A.D., were mostly about the ancient Roman Empire: conquests, invasions, battles, persecution of Christians, multiple Emperors, split into two Empires of West and East (on the site of Greek Byzantium), Constantinople founded, first Roman Catholic Popes, the first Bible organized, adjustment of calendars, and ultimately – the fall of the ancient Roman Empire and establishment of the new Christian Empire.

The Roman Empire began its decline with Pluto in Capricorn, split into two Empires with Pluto in Aquarius (300's), and transformed into the new Christian Empire with Pluto in Scorpio (500's).

The Birth of Jesus of Nazareth

One of the most significant events of the past two millenniums was the birth, life and death of Jesus of Nazareth. He has remained the most influential figure throughout the last 2,000 years, and continues into the third millennium.

Jesus' image has been at the center of all major events around the world: the Christian era was named after him; the calendar was adjusted on His account, persecutions and wars have been fought in His name, and the rest, "it's history."

According to historical records and astronomical indications, Jesus was born in 6 B.C. during a cycle of Pluto in Virgo. The reader will find this very suitable after reading in this book the Virgo Mass Movements. (Virgo is the opposite sign of Pisces).

The most probable date of the crucifixion, according to historians, was between 26 and 30 A.D. This is interesting, due to the fact that at the time of His death and alleged resurrection, or rebirth, Pluto was in Scorpio. Crucifixions were a common practice by the Romans during their occupation of Palestine. This will also be better understood after reading the Scorpio Mass Movements in this book.

Considering the overwhelming influence of Jesus throughout the last two millenniums of the Pisces Age, His birth chart and horoscope interpretation are included in this book, in addition to detailed accounts of the circumstances surrounding His birth (pages 99-108).

Pluto Cycles

1	2	3
♒ 305-329	♍ 1464-1479	♈ 1822-1852
♑ 532-551	♎ 1478-1491	♉ 1851-1883
♈ 600-633	♏ 1490-1503	♊ 1882-1913
♑ 778-796	♐ 1502-1516	♋ 1912-1939
♓ 1062-1089	♑ 1516-1532	♌ 1938-1958
	♒ 1532-1553	♍ 1957-1972
♌ 1201-1220	♓ 1552-1578	♎ 1971-1984
♍ 1218-1233	♈ 1577-1607	♏ 1983-1995
♎ 1232-1244	♉ 1606-1639	♐ 1995-2008
♏ 1243-1256	♊ 1638-1670	♑ 2008-2024
♐ 1256-1270	♋ 1668-1694	♒ 2023-2043
♑ 1269-1287	♌ 1692-1712	♓ 2043-2067
♒ 1286-1308	♍ 1710-1725	♈ 2066-2096
♓ 1307-1333	♎ 1724-1737	♉ 2095-2128
♈ 1332-1363	♏ 1736-1749	♊ 2127-2159
♉ 1362-1395	♐ 1748-1762	
♊ 1395-1425	♑ 1762-1778	♋ 2158-
♋ 1423-1448	♒ 1777-1798	♐ 2256-
♌ 1445-1466	♓ 1797-1822	♓ 2315-

Cycles of Pluto in Sagittarius

Keywords

Religion, Beliefs, Judgment, Supremacy, Law, Idealism, Adventure, Morality, Publicity, Theory, Influence, Travel, Foreign, Ethnic.

Ruler: Jupiter

Faith, Optimism, Expansion, Luck, Privilege, Fortune, Abundance, Benefits, Growth.

Past (1256-1270)

During this Sagittarius Mass Movement the Aztecs, a powerful and cultured people, migrated from the north to settle in the Valley of Mexico. They were the dominant civilization at the time of the Spanish conquest. Marco Polo, Italian traveler and merchant began his journeys to China. His memoirs had a tremendous influence in stimulating European interest in the Far East.

In medieval Italy, Thomas Aquinas entered the new Dominican order of the Roman Catholic Church. Scholastic professor, advisor at the papal court, and founder of the official

1

Catholic philosophy, he became the most influential philosopher of his time.

His metaphysics relied on Aristotelian concepts, thus he vindicated Aristotle against those who saw him as an inspiration of Averroism and heresy. Among his greatest works: "Summa contra Gentiles" and "Summa Theologica" immortalized Thomas Aquinas and are still extensively studied. Later he was canonized and became one of the principal saints of the Roman Catholic Church.

During this time, Moslems from North Africa were migrating to Europe. They mostly settled around Spain and Eastern Europe, where they later established the Ottoman Empire.

Past (1502-1516)

This Sagittarius Mass Movement brought the first European migration to the new world during the Spanish Inquisition, which started in Spain and spread throughout Europe. During this religious persecutions conducted by Roman Catholic tribunals, those who refused to convert to the faith were sentenced to death by burning.

During this cycle Michelangelo was painting the Sistine Chapel ceiling under the patronage of Pope Julius II. Raphael, another great artist of the Renaissance was painting the Vatican Palace in classical fresco—human figures in space.

At the end of this cycle Martin Luther, a German monk, began his crusade against the teachings and practices of the Roman Catholic Church. He deplored the financial exploitation of the people by the Church, challenged the sacraments and

2

denied the infallibility of popes and councils. Martin Luther was the catalyst that brought about the Protestant Reformation movement.

Past (1748-1762)

This Sagittarius Mass Movement brought the next big migration to the new world during the peak of the Protestant Reformation in Europe. This time Catholics, Puritans and other Christian sects, including the Freemason society, were being persecuted and expelled from Europe.

They were the first American colonists that in order to prevent the same from happening again, legislated the stipulation for religious freedom in the American constitution. Having experienced the perils of religion involved with government, they made the separation of Church and State a main priority in the new country.

Note: Religion and politics go hand-in-hand, especially during Sagittarius Mass Movements. When faith and religion get empowered by the influence of Pluto, it promotes a massive revival.

This represents a great opportunity for ambitious politicians and religious authorities seeking ultimate power, to seize the moment. This is when religion could make a difference between political winners and losers.

In the words of the great Greek philosopher Aristotle, "A tyrant must put on the appearance of uncommon devotion to religion—subjects do less easily move against him, believing that he has the gods on his side."

This philosophy, or strategy might win them the battle, but lose them the war. Falling out of grace is usually the end result.

Persecutions and massacres that begin while Pluto is in Scorpio are always followed by ethnic-religious conflicts and massive migrations with Pluto in Sagittarius.

Present and Future (1995–2008)

During this Sagittarius Mass Movement there are worldwide migrations of refugees as ethnic and religious fundamentalist groups compete for supremacy. Christians in Bosnia-Herzegovina backed by Belgrade, began a military campaign to force Muslims and Croats out of the Serb areas and isolate Sarajevo. Peacekeeping U.N. troops were pushed to the sidelines unable to stop the brutal eradication of an entire heritage.

The genocide spread over to Kosovo as Serbs attempted to annihilate an entire nation of Moslems and take over their land. This genocide prompted NATO and U.S. warplanes to intervene in the "ethnic cleansing" conflict and successfully stopped the bloodshed. However, peace in the region has remained unresolved.

Five years after the Kosovo war, international intervention and billions of dollars in aid have not calmed the hatred between Serbs and ethic Albanians. Ethnic violence has been escalating again as Albanians in Kosovo set Serbian Orthodox churches ablaze. In retaliation, rioters in the capital of Belgrade set a 17th century mosque on fire and another one was burned in the city of Nis. The mob chanted "death to all Kosovo Albanians."

Similar circumstances exist between India and Pakistan. Old rivalries between Hindus and Moslems continue to prevent both countries from realizing their full economic and geopolitical potential. Beginning in 1995 militant groups proceeded to systematically target Hindu communities. In their fight for the valley of Kashmir, these two mortal enemies came to the brink of nuclear war during the late '90s.

In America, followers of the white supremacist "Christian Identity religion," which is rabidly anti-abortion, anti-gay and anti-Semitic were accused of bombing women's health clinics and gay/lesbian nightclubs. The bombings caused multiple injuries and deaths. The self-proclaimed "Armies of God" Evangelical Christians were also responsible for killing doctors, nurses, and for harassing their patients and family members.

During this Sagittarius cycle the anti-government militia movement in America were eagerly training for the "apocalypse." When the former U.S. soldier, Tim McVeigh responded to the patriot rhetoric rage by bombing the Murrah Federal Building in Oklahoma City killing 168 people, right-wing doomsayers saw him as a leading horseman of the apocalypse. After McVeigh's execution in 2001 and after the new presidential elections, which robbed the movement of their favorite democratic villains, the militia membership began to plummet.

The new Millennium began with the most controversial elections in the history of USA. The highest court in the land—the Sagittarius ruled Supreme Court, took an unprecedented initiative to select a U.S. President against the will of the majority. This event made big headlines around the world, not only because it concerned the only super-power left in the world, but also because the news media, ruled by Sagittarius, has become more powerful than ever.

The Federal Communication Commission (FCC) is changing the old established laws on diversity in the media, in order to allow mighty moguls to monopolize the American national media.

Old religious and ethnic hatreds resurfaced between Israelis and Palestinians in the Middle East. Palestinian suicide bombings escalated against Israel and they in turn declared war against the Palestinians. Islamic terrorism in the name of God spread over against America. This was apparently in retaliation against U.S. support for Israel and American presence in Saudi Arabia.

Islamic suicide bombers hijacked and crashed U.S. commercial planes into the World Trade Twin Towers in New York City and the Pentagon in Washington DC. The third target was the Capitol, but passengers intervened and the plane blew up over Pennsylvania. It was the worst U.S. tragedy since the Japanese attack on Pearl Harbor in 1941.

These tragic terrorist acts caused the enforcement of new immigration laws and restrictions of civil liberties; the Patriot Act was designed to do just that. In addition, the U.S. government declared war against the Islamic fundamentalist al Qaida organization and Taliban leader Osama bin Laden in Afghanistan. American and British troops readily occupied Afghanistan. USA also declared a pre-emptive war against the leader of Iraq under the assumption that if they didn't destroy his regime first, some day he would attack Israel and America. In order to get public support for the war effort they accused him of possessing weapons of mass destruction.

6

While no such weapons were found, the American occupation of Iraq has suffered a significant amount of casualties, including thousands of Iraqis, other foreign troops and journalists. It is costing America about one billion a week and it looks like there's no end in sight. The hope is to recover some of the loss with oil revenues. Nevertheless, during a Sagittarius cycle Iraq is more likely to turn into an Islamic State than a modern democracy. The British tried it during their previous occupation of Iraq (1917-58) and failed. Iraqis finally overthrew the British-friendly installed monarchy with a violent coup.

Meanwhile, American military aggression in the region is being interpreted as a new Christian crusade against Islam. In addition, there is eminent threat of civil war on account of dissension among various religious and ethnic groups competing for control in the region. The Iraq conflict has revived intense religious sentiments around the world, as well as serious divisions among the American people at a national level.

As this Sagittarius Mass Movement progresses, we can expect religious and ethnic conflicts to escalate. This time, however, the migration of refugees is being curtailed, as most countries' capacity for asylum is already overwhelmed.

At present, there is chaos in the Caribbean nation of Haiti. After a violent revolt that ousted the former Catholic priest and Haitian president, he vowed to sue the U.S. and France for engineering his "political kidnapping." While in exile in a Central African Republic, President Aristide urged his supporters to resist the U.S. "occupation." U.S. troops in Haiti could do little to stop the spiral of violence. The U.S. President warned the Haitian people not to seek asylum in the USA, and ordered the Coast Guard to expatriate all the refugees.

During this Sagittarius Mass Movement Christian fundamentalists in the Republican Administration are implementing laws based on theocracy. The new "faith-based initiatives," which directs public funds to religious organizations has drastically lowered the constitutional wall separating Church and State. In addition, they are instigating the fulfillment of Biblical prophecies, according to their own interpretations thus antagonizing more hostility among other religious and ethnic groups.

The Republican Administration has declared a world crusade to pursue "the evil doers." The President specifically named the countries he accused of being "the axis of evil." It is beginning to look more like the old Christian Roman Empire than a modern Democracy.

The super-idealism and unquestionable faith inspired by Sagittarius can lead people into believing they have a monopoly on God's blessings hence "the ends justify the means." The current Sagittarius Mass Movement could regress civilization back to medieval ideological monopolies and holy wars.

Most Europeans realize they've "been there, done that" many times over and are reluctant to support America's new policies. Naturally, Europeans learned from their long bloody history of religious conflicts, so now prefer diplomatic negotiations.

America's strong Sagittarian identity is evident in the amount of Christian missionaries who travel around the world in search of converts. Although not legislated into law, being Christian, especially Protestant, and attending church is a prerequisite for becoming a U.S. president. There are more Christian churches in America than in the entire world, and most of them are wealthier than many countries.

America is also known as the land of opportunity and by the benevolent, optimistic and expansive nature of its people. Thus, the negative side of Sagittarius manifests through overdoing, over-reaching, arrogance and prejudice.

The Ku Klux Klan and other supremacist militia groups are perfect examples of American bigotry. In recent years the political organization the Christian Coalition has become the new supremacist power behind the Republican Administration. America is now being identified as a "Christian Nation." The multi-ethnic, multi-religious, and freedom-loving Democracy that made the country great is being threatened.

Dictating and moralizing in other international forums is changing America's world image, as well as deviating its destiny from its original ideal path for freedom and Democracy. In the mist of morality issues, the truth is difficult to recognize.

The meaning of truth is another prominent Sagittarian issue. Thus, truth is an abstract concept and as such, its search should remain an eternal pursuit. However, the major monotheistic religions claiming to have found the "ultimate truth" have stopped looking any further.

All sides are truly convinced that God is on their side. Now the cycle of Pluto in Sagittarius is challenging humanity to find out the truth by his/her own self, as the pertinent issues continue to escalate.

Pluto in Sagittarius is giving the world new opportunities to transform the old issues of religious zealotry and ethnic divisions. Pluto exposes into the open what has become repetitive in the same destructive ways.

Tolerance and fairness are the only hope towards freedom, growth and prosperity. And without freedom of thought, there's no freedom at all. With population exploding and limited living space left on the globe, it's imperative to respect everyone's God-given right to exist with dignity, regardless of creed, race, or nationality.

The old fundamentalist belief of destroying the infidel, or whoever happens to be the enemy, is not only delusional it is political suicide that sooner, or later backfires. Using religion to maintain blind confidence from the faithful cannot get far in these intellectually advanced times.

With worldwide instant communication, tyrannical actions to oppress people, or take over their territories, become an exercise in futility even during a religious fundamentalist cycle. Thus, the time has come to realize that the Biblical term, "an eye, for an eye" when applied, "leaves everyone blind" (Gandhi).

The United Nations Organization, which is the embodiment of an evolved Sagittarian concept, will be very much in the spotlight throughout this movement. Pluto is now emphasizing the fact that the world has become a global community, what affects one, affects all. Thus, it is imperative to maintain a unanimous effort towards the ultimate good of the whole—Earth and humanity.

Ironically, fundamentalist Christians in America have only contempt for the U.N. They expend a great deal of effort and resources on propaganda against the U.N. They are paranoid about the possibility of a "one world government" that some day will put them out of business.

The energy of Sagittarius has a propensity for extremes and the idealism to identify with the highest, which is testimony to the emphasis on God in America. These attitudes become more prominent during a Sagittarius Mass Movement.

During this Sagittarius Movement fundamentalist Christians in America have become so organized as to impose their religious views on the rest of the population. In many public schools around the country they have banned the science of evolution and replaced it with creationism. They have forced bible readings and prayer groups in the public schools at the exclusion of other religions.

Islamic groups in U.S. and Europe are also demanding similar rights. They are challenging secular laws that prohibit wearing traditional religious garments in state run schools, in addition to other government requirements. Before this religious movement is over, controversies over religion vs. secular laws could reach dangerous levels.

The Passion of the Christ (2004)

A new controversy has arisen with the release of the movie "The Passion of the Christ." Evangelical Christians are fervently promoting the movie and predicting it will encourage a massive conversion to Christianity. Meanwhile, the Jewish community is claiming the movie will arouse an increase of anti-Semitism. They accuse the movie of re-enforcing the old Christian propaganda that Jews killed Jesus Christ.

Jews are asking for the truth to be revealed once and for all; The Roman Empire ruled Jerusalem at the time and Roman soldiers led Jesus to his death. According to the first-century historian Josephus, Pontius Pilate was far from being the benign figure puzzled by the high priests' insistence on punishing Jesus. Pilate was rather a notoriously harsh prefect, quick to crucify even potential political rebels.

The fact that Jesus' arrival in the city stirred up popular interest among the holiday crowds in Jerusalem would have set off Pilate's alarms that he might be dealing with a seditious leader. The Jewish high priests of the Temple were also certainly concerned about any disturber of the peace, although declaring oneself the Messiah was not blasphemy by Jewish law.

According to Geza Vermes, emeritus professor of Jewish studies at Oxford University, if Jesus' crime had truly been blasphemy, as Gibson's movie asserts, the priests would have rightfully condemned Jesus to death by stoning rather than hand him over to Pilate for the Crucifixion, which was a specifically political punishment. In this case Roman concerns exceeded priestly ones.

Jesus and his followers simply saw themselves as a charismatic branch of Judaism—the wonder-working holy men of the time. Even the Gospel of Mark shows Jesus sharing the Pharisees' belief that love of one God and of one's fellow man are the greatest commandments. Their only divide was between the Jewish emphasis on the law and Jesus' emphasis on the spirit and grace.

These gentiles-in-Christ were writing the Gospels during the dramatic afterglow of the Jewish revolt of 66-74 A.D. and the Roman's destruction of the Second Temple. It would have been unwise and counterproductive for these creative writers to claim that Rome was responsible for killing a Jewish redeemer. This might have prompted Matthew to blame his own people, the Jews.

It is common knowledge the Roman Empire never held any sympathy for the first Christians. For over three centuries after the Crucifixion, Romans continued persecuting and killing the followers of Jesus, who were mostly Jews like him. Rome did not adopt Jesus as their savior until after the Empire began its decline.

In 312 A.D., Constantine, one of the four Caesars at the time, reputedly had a vision that led to his conversion. In 324 fighting under the insignia of the cross, Constantine defeated his last rival to become the emperor of the new Roman Christian Empire. Constantine convened the Council of Nicaea, where at least 250 bishops met to formulate the official articles of faith including Jesus' place in the Holy Trinity, in the first Nicene Creed.

Bishops who disagreed with the creed were promptly exiled. Under his regime, Sunday became the Christian Sabbath, Christians were told not to confer with the rabbis on the date of Easter, and any Jew who obstructed the conversion of another to Christianity was put to death.

As the Roman Empire went Christian, Jesus was increasingly seen as the divine incarnation of the second person of the Trinity and less as a Jew from Nazareth. In the words of Amy-Jill Levine, professor at Vanderbilt Divinity School, "when his Judaism was noted, it was only to say that he 'was rejected by his own' or that he 'came to demolish the old system from within." The notion that Jesus' purpose was to destroy Judaism contradicts the Bible statements that He did not come to destroy the law; He came "to fulfill it."

During the current Sagittarius Mass Movement Angels paraphernalia became the latest fad in America. Christian bookstores are a highly profitable enterprise. Apocalyptic thrillers and other Christian books are the best sellers. There has been a dramatic crossover of Christian pop culture to secular mainstream markets including music, TV shows and movies. Book clubs about religious subjects and prophesy; fiction and non-fiction have become a social phenomenon.

Another significant event typical of a Sagittarius cycle was the rise and fall of the "Higher Source Cult," or "Heaven's Gate." These cultists could be called members of a pastiche, millennial, sectarian religion made of many strands of beliefs from all the world's faiths. Led by their charismatic, grandiose and paranoid leader, Marshall Applewhite, they believed to be extraterrestrial spiritual beings whose true home was in a higher dimension or galaxy. In 1997 the 39 cult members committed suicide by simultaneously drinking a poison, while believing their souls would blissfully clutch to the tale of the Hale-Bobb comet, which would take them back to the higher level they had come from.

The latest and most violent ethnic and religious conflict is taking place in the African Sudan. Since February 2003, an ethnically Arab militia of horse-mounted bandits called the Janjaweed have destroyed villages, killed tens of thousands of black Africans and displaced more than 1.4 million. These militiamen receive financial and military support from the Sudanese government and were commissioned by them to put down an insurgency by the region's non-Arab Muslims.

The United Nations says the pogrom has created the worst

humanitarian disaster in the world today. Hundreds of refugees are dying of disease every day and tens of thousands are expected to die by the end of the year. Meanwhile, there seems to be global paralysis in the face of this large-scale ethnic cleansing in Africa—despite the fact that the international Genocide Convention, signed by the U.S. and 134 other countries, obligates signatories to "prevent and punish" genocide where it is occurring.

Opposition to sanctions has come from Arab countries that are sympathetic to Khartoum and from other Security Council members that are heavily invested in Sudan's emerging oil industry. This has forced the U.S. to scale back a resolution that would punish Khartoum should it fail to halt the killing.

This Sagittarius Mass Movement heralds a time when dramatic religious and ethnic controversies reach a dangerous climax. The fact that the Pisces Age of delusion is in its last phase exacerbates the problem. Many people are still unable to perceive the truth from lies and deception. Even as the turmoil energized by Pluto leads to long-term resolutions, it is mostly dependent on the level of awareness and effort to compromise exerted by the people involved.

Sagittarius Generation (1995-2008)

The children born during these extreme philosophically divisive times are the innocent victims of ingrained prejudices and religious fanaticism, which plagued civilization since its primitive beginnings. Some will become the future enforcers of the "old time religion." Thus, like other Sagittarius generations before, some will aspire to correct the mistakes of the past and reach higher than the last.

They are the future daring adventurers, who will go "where no man has gone before" in order to break the barriers that separate people. They will aim at transforming dogma and creed into wisdom turning the superficial into the super- conscious. This group will begin to impact world governments during the next Aquarius (2023-43) and Pisces (2043-67) Mass Movements.

The new Americas were the last frontier in the past millennium. By the time Pluto returns to Sagittarius again in about 248 years after 2008 (2256), SPACE will be the final frontier. The Sagittarius spirit of exploration reflected by the NASA Space Program will continue to aim its arrow at the heavens in search of new horizons; "the sky is the limit" for the Sagittarius archer.

Not surprisingly, during the present Sagittarius cycle (1995-2008), the Space Program reached its height, as well as its low. They built a manned Space Station and the space shuttle made a myriad of successful flights. They also suffered two tragic explosions:

The shuttle Columbia explosion of February 2003 occurred on its way back after a successful mission, as it entered the earth atmosphere high over the skies of Texas. It was the first time the shuttle had taken an Israeli astronaut into space.

The previous explosion of the Challenger occurred in January 1986 soon after takeoff. It was the first time the space shuttle was taking a woman schoolteacher into space.

Even as these tragic accidents stopped the manned missions temporarily, nothing will deter the Sagittarius spirit from continuing aiming upwards. In 2003, the Hubble telescope focused its powerful digital camera at a patch of the sky to capture a photo image of what's known as the Hubble Ultra Deep Field. It produced a vivid portrait of the early days of the universe. With representative pictures greatly magnified, the model marks the location of some 200,000 galaxies, each with many billions of stars. The images delighted cosmologists who study the origin and evolution of the universe. They say their science is graduating from an era of theory to an era of visible data.

Scientists are collecting the photo album of the life history of the universe for the first time: "the baby pictures, the teenage pictures, the grown-up pictures." Fueling the creation of realistic simulations are supercomputers using dozens of linked processors and computational techniques from nuclear weapons laboratories. They can now compare the pictures of theory with those of nature.

In addition, NASA has recently successfully landed a few unmanned rovers on the surface of Mars. They analyzed Martian soil and rocks for chemical and mineral composition. Equipped with amazing panoramic cameras, they were able to take spectacular images of the terrain and beam them home—often in 3-D.

The current U.S. President proposed a future manned moon mission, with the goal of a moon base to serve as a launching pad for a mission to Mars. This is a very futuristic big idea—an optimistic one, typical of a Sagittarius Mass Movement.

Cycles of Pluto in Capricorn

Keywords

Business, Authority, Ambition, Convention, Administration, Government, Conservative, Snobbish, Prudish, Parental, Methodical.

Ruler: Saturn

Responsibility, Discipline, Limitation, Rigidity, Fear, Respect, Repression, Restriction, Order.

Past (532-551)

After the final disintegration of the ancient Roman Empire, this was a transitional period into the new Christian Orthodox Byzantine Empire. The great Byzantine Emperor Justinian I recovered much of the lost territory in the West and was also responsible for the codification of the Roman Civil Laws, "Justinian's Code." He issued an edict condemning the writings of the early Greek theologian Origen, and had the entire Bible revised. He also closed the 1000-year-old School of Philosophy in Athens. The Byzantine Empire was at height.

Past (778-796)

This Capricorn Mass Movement brought the second ecumenical council of the Roman Catholic Church in Nicaea, Asia Minor. In this juncture, the Church abandoned iconoclasm and ordered the veneration of images. Emperor Constantine imprisoned his mother Irene for cruelty.

The king of the Franks by succession, Charlemagne, French for "Charles the Great," began his conquests throughout Europe. His domain was extended to include rule over France, the Netherlands, Belgium, Germany, Austria, Italy, Spain, the Saxons and the Holy Roman Emperors. Byzantine Empress Irene, mother of Constantine, proposed marriage to Charlemagne after she blinded her son and assumed sole power of the empire. Charlemagne's coronation as Emperor by Pope Leo III revived the imperial office in the West and established a connection between the Papacy and the monarchy (Church and State). This connection was to be of prime importance in the history of medieval Europe (the Greek Church later canonized Irene).

Past (1269-1287)

This Capricorn Movement brought about the year of the 4 Popes (1276), Gregory X, Innocent V, Hadrian V and John XXI. Christians hanged 278 Jews for clipping coin—even as they were guilty of the same (counterfeiting). The Asen dynasty in Bulgaria was extinguished and became subject to Serbs, Greeks, and Mongols. Kublai Khan founded the Yuan dynasty in China. The Teutonic Order completed the subjection of Prussia, Germany. Genoa defeated Pisa, and the French were massacred in Sicily. Giovanni Campanella, mathematician and chaplain to Pope Urban IV, devised the Campanus System of Houses, a new method of house divisions for horoscope calculations still in use today.

Past (1516-1532)

During this cycle Erasmus published the New Testament with Greek and Latin text. Martin Luther's protest against the Church set in motion the Reformation movement in Germany. He was summoned by Cardinal Cajetan and advised to write a letter of submission to Pope Leo X, or face excommunication. Luther promised to do it, but recanted after questioning the infallibility of papal decisions. England's Queen Mary I, called "Bloody Mary" initiated religious persecutions of Protestants resulting in the martyrdom of 300.

Spanish conquistadors and other European explorers were navigating the globe acquiring territories. They built forts in the Caribbean, S. America, Mexico, Florida. The exploitation of African slaves and the trade of commodities, such as coffee, sugar, indigo, cotton, and silk, took off. European imperialistic kingdoms were fighting over the new territories and ample resources.

The popular book at this time was *The Prince*, a guide to power politics by Italian politician and historian, Niccolo Machiavelli. His infamous ideas of "dominionism" made an impact upon world leaders throughout his lifetime and thereafter to a long line of kings, ministers and tyrants, such as Mussolini, Hitler, Lenin, Stalin.

Machiavelli taught that it is dangerous for leaders to practice goodness; instead, they must pretend to be good and then do the opposite. "Everybody sees what you appear to be, few feel what you are, and those few will not dare to oppose themselves to the many, who have the majesty of the state to defend them; and in the actions of men, and especially of princes, from which there is no appeal, the end justifies the means."

Past (1762-1778)

This Capricorn Mass Movement caused European imperialism to reach its zenith. Church and State were one. Monarchs, aristocrats and clergy were living off of the poor and oppressed. The new American colony initiated the Revolutionary War against England's King George III, leading to the Declaration of Independence and the creation of the United States Constitution. This cycle gave birth to Napoleon Bonaparte, future Emperor of France.

Note: The test of power can be most severe in the sign of Capricorn. Pluto here purges and cleanses the materialistic selfishness inherent in the drive for power. Capricorn is the sign of government systems and earthy ambitions inclusive of the drive for respect, recognition and status.

The altruistic purpose of Capricorn is to climb the ladder of success in order to make a meaningful contribution to society. When privileges are righteously earned and graciously shared they multiply, otherwise the top of the mountain can be a very lonely and meaningless dead-end with one alternative left—the downfall.

Future (2008-2024)

This Mass Movement will impact the new American monarchies: Big business (corporate empires), church, and state, which by this time are one-and-the-same. With one group at the top holding absolute power and the gap between rich and poor converted into a schism, national security will tighten. Censorship, fear and depression will prevail.

The trends that are evident during the Sagittarius cycle will continue. By this time conservative forces in government will have privatized most federal agencies. Federal funds and authority will continue to be transferred to churches in charge of the school system and other social services.

With government deregulation and privatization, most state and local administrations are left to run their own exclusive theoretical kingdoms. The implementation of conservative and biblical laws that began during the Sagittarius cycle will continue. Basic civil rights will be oppressed, especially women's.

The Republican Administration began replacing moderate and liberal judges with ultra-conservative ones, and attempted to amend the constitution accordingly. Federal and local governments were gradually dismantling the public system, especially in education. They continued closing agencies and programs that mostly benefited the poor. The impact of this new system will be strongly felt at this time.

People will still be demoralized from the collapse of some corporate empires early in the new millennium. There is high unemployment from corporate cost reductions, bankruptcies, massive layoffs and American companies moving jobs to third-world countries for higher profits.

The policies of tax cuts designed mainly to benefit the very wealthy; the rise in spending on national security and keeping up with wars, depleted the economy and drastically increased the national debt. And as usual, those deficits always fall on the backs of the common people.

This will be Pluto's first return to Capricorn since the birth of USA. America's Pluto in Capricorn in the second house of material resources and values lived up to its powerful expectations—America became the wealthiest and most powerful country in the world.

Unfortunately, the policy of unilateralism, arrogant nationalism and imperialism has caused anti-Americanism around the world. This could lead to isolationism—not to mention more terrorism. This period marks the zenith of the new American Empire.

Exacerbating the problems will be Pluto in Capricorn making an opposition to the U.S. Cancer Sun. This is indicative of a major turning point for the USA. The last time Pluto was in Capricorn the American people revolted against imperial England and King George III.

As Pluto's return begins to resurface the old issues, it will resuscitate the need to reestablish original constitutional principles that will cause the reevaluation of materialistic and imperialistic values. By this time the overall damage to the country could be so great, recovery will be a difficult challenge.

The same also applies to other countries with similar records. Pluto's energy promotes a powerful rise to the top, but when that power is misused and abused, the fall can be devastating. This time will be reminiscence to the fall of previous empires at different times in history.

Saturn, ruler of Capricorn demands a high price to pay when

earth's precious resources, including humans, are used irresponsibly for personal power and material gain. Saturn teaches that injustice creates enemies, enemies create fear, and fear is the enemy of prosperity.

At this time the prospects for the world will look grim until the process of transformation, regeneration, and healing, also inspired by Pluto, take its course.

Capricorn Generation (2008-2024)

This Capricorn Mass Movement will give birth to a new generation of ambitious politicians and future business, government and religious administrators, who will be ready to establish new government structures during the future Aries Mass Movement (2066-96). Some will become corrupted by power; others will emulate the previous Forefathers, or Framers of the U.S. Constitution.

These prolific men were Freemasons, who believed in one universal God, architect and creator of the universe. Their vision for America was humanitarian and inclusive. Obviously, they never set out to create a "Christian Nation," as evangelists falsely claim. This is evident by the fact that Jesus, or Christianity were never mentioned in any of the official documents. Clearly, they considered every human being as a child of God, contrary to Christianity, which sees Jesus as "God's only son." Future generations will finally recognize the difference.

Cycles of Pluto in Aquarius

Keywords

Diversity, Humanism, Revolution, Reform, Progress, Individualism, Independent groups, Intellectuality, Science, Technology, Invention.

Ruler: Uranus

Unpredictable, Unconventional, Rebellious, Unique, Original, Eccentric, Erratic, Change.

Past (305-329)

During this Aquarius Mass Movement Romans declared an end to the persecution of Christians. The Roman Empire split into two empires of West and East, and Emperor Constantine finally established toleration of Christianity.

The first council of Nicaea by the Roman Catholic and Eastern Orthodox churches convened. Roman Emperor Constantine settled a dispute and declared the divinity of Christ and fixed the date of Easter. Also at this time, the Jews improved their calendar by introducing different lengths of years. In the Roman Empire, Emperor Julian the Apostate

27

was attempting to revive paganism in the Empire (the worship of many Gods, mostly named after the planets).

Past (1286-1308)

This cycle brought an Alliance between France and Scotland. There were treaties between Venice and the Turks, and France with Germany. There was a temporary end of European slave trade. Marco Polo returned to Italy and began to dictate his extraordinary memoirs. Spectacles were invented and the first medical reference to spectacles was made. Urine examination became means of medical diagnosis.

Osman defeated the Byzantines marking the end of Christian rule in East Europe. The new Moslem Ottoman Empire was established. They conquered Constantinople, Anatolia and the Balkans. Moslem "holy wars" against Christians created panic throughout central Europe. The new Moslem empire ruled Eastern Europe for 600 years until WWI. They also ruled Spain for over seven centuries until the Inquisition.

Past (1532-1553)

During this Aquarius Mass Movement the Inquisition began in Portugal. Portuguese immigrants colonized Brazil. Spanish explorer Francisco Pizarro executed the Inca of Peru. Clergy Ignatius Loyola founded the Jesuit Order. Martin Luther completed the translation of the Bible into German and the Protestant Reformation spread into France, Denmark, Norway and Scotland. The Authority of the Pope was void in England. Luther stated Catholics were like Jews, only worse. After failing to convert the Jews to his new form of Christianity, he retaliated by publishing "On the Jews and Their Lies"

(1543). The ambivalence about Jesus' Jewishness became most evident. For its part, the Catholic Church declared that all sinners bore the burden of Christ's death, even while it imposed new restrictions on "unbelievers."

The "great comet" (later Halley's) aroused a wave of superstition. Fontana initiated the science of ballistics called "Tartaglia." Servetus discovered pulmonary circulation of the blood. And in confirmation of the correlation between insanity and genius (Aquarius), the first lunatic asylums were opened.

One of the most significant discoveries during this Aquarius cycle was by Corpernicus, who formulated the order of the Solar System. This Polish church official and astronomer established the Sun at the center of the Universe, with Earth and planets revolving in periodic orbits. New texts were published in Arithmetic, cosmography, philosophy, anatomy, geography, and more. Aureolus Paracelsus, a Swiss-German physician and scientist, created a manual of astrology, "Grosse Astronomie."

The French doctor/astrologer and prophet of his age, Nostradamus, made his first predictions (1547). At this time astrology was only permitted in the Church and Courts. Astrology magazines were printed with recommendations as to when to plant, harvest, bathe, marry, travel, etc. These were a luxury only for the rich and powerful; besides, most poor people were illiterate.

Geographer G. Mercator did the first map of Flanders; using the name America for the first time, and also stated the earth has a magnetic pole. Olaus Magnus did the first map of the world.

Past (1777-1798)

During this Aquarius Mass Movement, soon after the Boston massacre and the American Revolution, the French Revolution took place (1789-99). A series of costly wars and feudal tax exemptions for the privileged had imposed heavy financial burdens levied upon the peasants and rising middle class. The church was linked to the monarchs and privileged hence was also regarded as corrupt. As poverty, distress and ignorance were widespread, the oppressed masses stormed the Bastille in an unparalleled social upheaval intended to topple the old imperial traditional system.

It ended with the massacre of hundreds of Royalists and public beheadings of the abusive monarchs—many clergy and nobles went abroad to escape the rising turmoil. The reformers' slogan was "Liberty, Equality, Fraternity."

In 1781, another revolutionary and significant event occurred with the discovery of the planet Uranus. In view of the planet's compatibility with the qualities of Aquarius (physically and figuratively), it was officially declared the new ruler of the sign. Interestingly enough, no one knew at the time Pluto was in Aquarius emphasizing the event.

Note: Pluto in Aquarius empowers the revolutionary spirit of humanity. It re-awakens the human need to express true individualism and originality. It encourages the need to brake free from rigid social patterning that limits individual potential. The struggle for liberty and social justice becomes uncontrollable.

Group power is necessary when defying the old suppressive structures. It is also imperative to have a true humanitarian purpose and new ideas in order to replace the outdated and outgrown. Change for the sake of change can turn into chaos.

When divisive fringe groups attempt to destabilize the established order, the larger and better-organized opposing forces always prevail. In Aquarius, all the powers on Earth cannot stop change and progress.

Future (2023-2043)

This Aquarius Mass Movement will give us a clear glimpse into the coming Age of Aquarius. This is a transitional time when the world will be experiencing the sunset of the Pisces Age and getting ready for the sunrise of the "New Age of Humanity."

At this particular juncture, people will begin to wake up and reclaim their God-given human rights. There will be turmoil and upheaval, as the old powerful suppressive forces struggle to retain control. Explosions will increase, as well as the potential for chemical and biological warfare.

After a period of instability, progressive groups will prevail leading to major government and social reforms. New independent political parties representing the common people (the masses) will come forth to replace the old traditional systems, especially in America. Imperialistic, fascist and totalitarian governments around the world will find it very difficult to survive during these tumultuous times.

This new intellectual awakening will act to break down the walls separating people and nations, so that every human being on earth will have the opportunity to realize his/her greatest potentials. New laws honoring civil rights regardless of gender, race, or creed will be implemented. Diversity and inclusiveness will be the new vogue.

There will be drastic changes regarding nuclear weapons, the environment, and the World Bank Organization. Genetic engineering aimed at helping humanity could become a common practice. Dynamic developments concerning the use of electric vehicles should be expected. There will be amazing new inventions and discoveries in general. This could be the onset of an advanced humanitarian, technological and scientific era.

This transitional process, however, will take at least another complete revolution of Pluto around the zodiac. In the meantime, revolutionary movements of diversified groups should be expected at this time.

The Aquarius Generation (2023-43)

This Aquarius Mass Movement will give birth to a generation of rebellious individuals, among them many "rebels without a cause"—due to an inner lack of true purpose. Others of this generation will become magnanimous social reformers and inventive geniuses. They will have the courage and wisdom to break up old rigid forms, in order to devise new trails toward lasting contributions to world progress.

Astronomical Facts: At the present time the Vernal Equinox, which marks the timing of the ages, has approximately five more degrees of the Pisces constellation left to cover, according to the experts on this field. For mathematical purposes, the constellations are divided into 12 sections consisting of 30 degrees each. Due to the fact that constellations have uneven boundaries, part of the Pisces constellation is within the

32

confines of Aquarius. (Refer to Zodiac Chart on page 98.) The Vernal Equinox moves about one degree of space every 72 years—a World Age consist of 2160 years. At the time of Jesus' birth in 6 B.C., the Age of Pisces was already in progress. By the 2150's the new Age of Aquarius will have officially begun and the new avatar for the Aquarius Age will be born (refer to the future Gemini Movement in this book).

Moses, the avatar of the ancient Aries Age, was a leader and a warrior (Aries). He was the architect and original enforcer of "God's laws."

Jesus, the avatar of the Pisces Age was a mystic and a martyr (Pisces). His spiritual message changed the world.

We should expect the avatar of the Aquarius Age to be an intellectual rebel and a champion for social justice, whose progressive ideas will revolutionize the world. This time around, humanity will rise up in heighten anticipation and will be readily awaiting the arrival of the Aquarian incarnation.

(Refer to *Defining Relationships Astrologically* by this author for a more extensive depiction on The New Age of Aquarius and other important astrological information. The keywords, color-coded, cutout cards included in the book provide additional comprehension of the symbolic language of astrology for better understanding of Pluto's cycle around the zodiac and its influence on world events—Mass Movements and the Generations).

33

Cycles of Pluto in Pisces

Keywords

Disappointment, Victimization, Dissolution, Illusion, Sacrifice, Persecution, Spirituality, Epidemics, Jails, Hospitals, Chemicals, Oil.

Ruler: Neptune

Inspiration, Devotion, Fantasy, Mysticism, Intuition, Introspection, Confusion, Delusion, Addiction, Defeat, Bondage.

Past (1062-1089)

This Pisces Mass Movement marked the onset of the Crusades. Initiated by Pope Urban II, Christians rampaged throughout Europe and the Middle East slaughtering millions of people in a fanatic quest for conversion. Bishop St. Anselm, friend of Pope Urban II argued in "Why God Became Man" that the Crucifixion atoned for the sins of humankind.

In the words of James Caroll, former Catholic priest, and author of *Constantine's Sword: The Church and the Jews*, "it was a time of plagues, savage war and millennial fever. The notion of Christ's sacrifice was a way of coping with a very violent and brutal world, and a way of making sense of it." In other words, it was a brilliant idea in behalf of the Roman Catholic Church to justify their own sins for the heinous crimes they were guilty of.

Christian warriors who joined the Crusades were promised remission of sins, immediate entry into paradise if they died, and protection of their property and position while they were in route to liberate the Holy Land. However, the soldiers stopped in the Rhineland, where they left up to a third of northern Europe's Jews dead.

The movement became known as the "Wars of the Cross" and their battle cry was "God wills it." Joining the Crusades was difficult to resist. Ultimately, after all the carnage, the Christian Crusades ended up as a complete failure.

Past (1307-1333)

The Christian Crusades that began in the previous Pisces cycle were finally called off. At its conclusion, the Holy Land was more in Moslem's hands than in the beginning. It was a futile attempt to free the Holy Land from Moslem domination. The Christian Crusaders were defeated by their own un-Christian and self-deluded methods of forced conversion.

Although the church officially condemned the attacks nothing stanched the ongoing anti-Jewish violence. Jews were falsely accused of "ritual murder," claiming they killed Christian boys to drink their blood at Passover as a re-enactment of the Crucifixion. Even the Bubonic plague that originated in India and the Black plague of the mid-1300s, which devastated Europe, were attributed to a "Jewish plot." The persecution of Jews spread throughout Germany and Russia.

During this Pisces Movement, Thomas Aquinas, the original founder of the Roman Catholic philosophy, was canonized in sainthood.

Past (1552-1578)

During this Mass Movement the Jesuits Order began founding Christian colleges around Europe. Jews were persecuted in Bavaria while the Zohar cabbalistic Jewish mysticism was printed.

At this time Nostradamus was the only physician in France giving his services for free to the poor during the plague epidemic. While under persecution by Church authorities, he did his astrological studies in secret and wrote his prophesies in seclusion. The French King and Queen, who took him to the palace to be their personal physician/advisor until his death, finally saved his life.

Puritanism was prevalent in England. The Elizabethan Prayer Book and the first English edition of the *Book of Martyrs* were published. The Church of Scotland was founded, and the Counter Reformation began. There were Multiple Wars of Religion in France. Astrology was banned and books were ordered burned.

Calvinists and other Protestant sects allied against Jesuits. England was a police State, and people were executed for religious reasons. American Tobacco and the habit of snuff were introduced in Europe.

The plague outbreak in Europe killed more than 20,000. The

fever epidemic killed 40,000 in Lisbon, the influenza epidemic took over Europe, and the typhoid fever killed two million Native American Indians.

Past (1797-1822)

During this Pisces cycle, Andrew Jackson organized the first genocidal slaughter of an Indian Nation. It led to "The Trail of Tears" when the Indian Shaman cursed the "Great White Father in Washington for broken promises." It became the infamous "Presidential Curse" of every 20 years (Presidents inaugurated on the Jupiter-Saturn conjunction died while in office – except for Reagan, who survived a gunshot due a mutation on the cycle. The remaining Indians were defeated, placed into Reservations, forced to accept a new religion and language, then many of them became addicted to alcohol. The congress of Vienna ended the Napoleonic Era. Napoleon died in exile from slow arsenic poisoning, as he claimed.

Note: Pisces is considered the last sign of the Zodiac. As a complete cycle of Pluto around the twelve signs of the Zodiac is concluded, all the materialistic mistakes of the past are confronted.

In Pisces humanity is forced to face karma, "as ye sowed, ye shall so reap." Pisces lessons are mainly about loss, sorrow, humility, deception, escapism and martyrdom. True compassion and spiritual awareness are the main objectives.

In the search for spirituality, the Pisces energy can be very vulnerable to blind belief blindly followed. This cycle offers the opportunity for introspection, reflection and rectification, so the sins of the past can be transcended and awaken to a new spiritual reality.

The key to enlightenment is found through introspection. In Jesus' words, "the kingdom of heaven is within you." He also advised, "go into your closet to pray." Those words suggest that through the subconscious mind we connect to our higher self, or Divine Intelligence.

Through the subconscious we have access to past lives' memories and knowledge. The only things we take with us after every lifetime is what we learned, which explains what we already know, but don't know why we know it. These past lives' assets are always available for the purpose of soul evolution. The soul merely picks up where it previously left off.

Jesus was the avatar of the Pisces Age that is now ending, but His highly evolved spiritual teachings somehow got lost in organized religion. Obviously, Jesus tried to convey the message that divine access requires no intermediaries.

The purpose of prayer, or meditation is to seek insights from within, in order to find balance and harmony—inner peace. Unfortunately, throughout the illusive Age of Pisces, prayer has been wrongly used for proselytizing: emotional, spiritual, and mental manipulation to convert. Repetition of mantras is scientifically proven successful in programming the subconscious mind. In the past these tactics were meant to encourage increased dependency, powerlessness and submission.

Unscrupulous agents still use these religious practices for self-aggrandizement and material gain. They make presumptuous claims of having God's personal advice and blessings bestowed upon them, as if God chose to favor them exclusively. Others simply suffer from confusion or mental delusion. The truly inspired individuals find no need for such deceiving claims.

The planet Neptune is our telepathic missing link. It is through this planet that we can access the purest creative energies of the universe. Where gifted artists get their inspiration and cannot explain where it's coming from, or how it happens. Through introspection we enrich our world of thought and reach out into new fields of knowledge and understanding. "Know thy self" first, in order to know others.

As Pluto empowers the energies of Pisces and Neptune, it promotes the need to unveil the illusions of the past that kept man in bondage. At this time humanity learns that God's love has no preferences and no boundaries; it is unconditional, it is universal.

Future (2043-2067)

This Pisces Mass Movement could bring final resolutions to petroleum dependency due to its depletion. The world will be suffering the consequences from environmental neglect and deterioration. By this time the rising sea levels as a result of Global Warming will be catastrophic.

Poison gases in the atmosphere may become unbearable and clean water will be a rare commodity. In addition, the world at this time will be facing the process of consolidating the transition from an era based on blind beliefs to an era based on enlightenment.

This Pisces Mass Movement will mark the beginning of the end of the Pisces Age that began before the first century of the "Christian Era." There could be final confrontations among the world's major religions, as they face the potential of total dissolution.

People will be confronting major disappointments and disillusionments about the past and could become vulnerable to new cults. There could be plagues, persecution, confusion, depression and chaos. The homeless and destitute will have increased to critical levels.

At the same time during this Pisces cycle, new spiritual truths will be perceived. New laws and methods for dealing with pollution and chemical addictions will be implemented. Pharmaceutical industries will go through major adjustments.

Charitable and medical institutions will be overhauled, including institutions of confinement. Drastic measures will be taken about the pollution of the oceans, as they try to exploit those resources to compensate for the depletions on Earth.

The Pisces Generation (2043-2067)

This Pisces Mass Movement will give birth to a generation of gifted visionaries and artists. Many enlightened spiritual gurus and inspired mystics born, will eventually lead the world into highly evolved spirituality and transcended levels of consciousness. Telepathy and other forms of psychic phenomena will be extensively explored.

This group will instinctually know that world peace begins within, and redemption cannot be achieved without first recognizing the divinity inherent in every living organism on earth. All of nature's kingdoms deserve to be honored and preserved, i.e., animal, vegetable and mineral. Furthermore, this evolved Pisces group will instinctually know that keeping people in bondage retards the collective evolutionary growth process of mankind.

Most importantly, this group will have an innate understanding about the meaning of, "Thy will, be done on earth, as it is (indicated) in heaven (sky)." The planets and constellations will never be seen again as merely physical objects devoid of meaning and purpose. The art/science of astrology will finally assume the respect and consideration it deserves, as this generation initiates its impact upon the world during the next Gemini Mass Movement.

Further Look into the Future Pisces Mass Movement of 2315

The next time Pluto returns to Pisces 248 years after 2067, the New Age of Aquarius will be in full swing hence the Pisces period will be highly creative and spiritually evolved. By this time reincarnation will be an accepted reality. "The truth that makes you free" will be finally assimilated in the human consciousness.

Awareness of the law of cause and effect (karma) encourages deterrence from destructiveness. The realization that every individual is personally responsible for his/her soul evolution—salvation, could be the only hope towards the survival of civilization.

At this point, there will be no more suicidal bombers seeking the illusion of "virgins in paradise." The perennial heaven and hell will no longer be used as excuses for reward and punishment. It will be very difficult for tyrants to mislead, deceive, or control.

This distant Pisces cycle promises to liberate humanity's soul from bondage once and for all. Enlightenment means: coming out of darkness, or seeing clearly through the fog of earthy confusion. Only then, can we follow the path to self-realization. This is when the soul rises above the personality hence the person ceases to be part of the materialistic and dogmatic theoretical "herd."

Self-realized individuals know they are the masters of their own fate and no longer blame God for everything—good or bad. As the illusive notions of a biased, vindictive and egocentric God become no longer feasible in people's minds, evil will be easier to eradicate. In addition, humility will replace arrogance by the privileged ones, who feel superior by the notion they have been personally "blessed" by God.

Realizing that they earned their privileges in a past life will deter them from taking their so called, "God's blessings" for granted. Instead, they could use their earned blessings to help humanity, as many advanced souls have done.

If Mother Theresa's soul came back totally endowed with wealth, luck, privileges, for no obvious reasons, using her gifts for self-aggrandizement and frivolous indulgences, her previous good works would have been a complete waste. In this case, she would come back next time with absolutely nothing and no hope for improvement. In cases of misused talents, the person would bring back those same talents, but efforts in finding a source of appreciation would be futile causing tremendous frustration. This is what "divine justice" is all about.

The Pisces energy offers humanity various choices: we can

choose to be the saviors of our own souls, or become the victims of unscrupulous tyrants. We can use our earned "blessings" for good or for evil. We can also choose escapism and self-undoing and waste an entire incarnation. So much of the world's vicissitudes during the Pisces age have been caused by the literal interpretation of Bibles. Many souls have been led astray by the glorification of victimization, martyrdom and violence encouraged in the name of God. Future generations will realize that the old stories and rules of past civilizations do not apply to modern times.

Pisces has been the fundamental motivational force behind every cycle of Pluto throughout the entire Pisces Age. Likewise, Aquarius will be the prevailing motivational influence behind all of Pluto's cycles during the future Aquarius Age. Emotional submission, due to blind devotion to religious beliefs—Pisces, will be replaced by intellectual and humanitarian awareness towards self-responsibility, freedom of thought, equality, and world progress—Aquarius.

Cycles of Pluto in Aries

Keywords

Independence, Assertion, Conviction, Liberty, Leadership, New Beginnings, Competition.

Ruler: Mars

Aggression, Action, Impulse, Passion, Anger, Challenge, Autonomy, Initiative, Courage, Physical, Drive, Energy, Directness.

Past (600-633)

During this Aries Mass Movement, Spain became an elective kingdom of the Visigoths. Tibet began to develop into a unitary state and Buddhism became the state religion.

The prophet Mohammed founded the religion of Islam after many battles and persecutions. He had his first vision on Mount Hira in 610, captured Mecca and dictated the Koran in 625, and died in 632 A.D. The Arabs attacked Persia (Iran), and Medina became the seat of Mohammedanism (Islam). Moslems also captured the Christian churches of Jerusalem, Antioch, Alexandria and the country of Spain.

Past (1332-1363)

This Aries cycle marked the zenith of Arabic civilization in Spain and the beginning of the Hundred Years' War in Europe.

Jews began to be persecuted in Germany, and Western Europe began building Monumental Cathedrals of Gothic art and architecture.

Past (1577-1607)

During this Aries Movement, Spain invaded Portugal. Russia conquered Siberia, and Ivan IV, "The Terrible," killed his son and heir with his own hands. The Gregorian calendar was adopted in Papal States. The Catacombs of Rome were discovered.

The Danish nobleman and mathematician Tycho Brahe, after discovering the first Supernova decided to give his life to astrology. The King of Denmark financed the observatory, and Tycho became imperial mathematician/advisor to the Holy Roman Emperor, Rudolph II.

After Tycho's death (1601), his German assistant mathematician, Johannes Kepler was appointed to continue Tycho's work. He developed the "Kepler's Laws" and became the founder of modern astronomy. He also developed the theory of optics.

During this cycle William Shakespeare was recognized as an actor and playwright. He wrote his greatest plays and built the largest theatre in England. Francis Drake proclaimed sovereignty of England. Roman Pope Sixtus V proclaimed a

Catholic Crusade to invade England. New buildings were banned in London to restrict growth of the city. Queen Elizabeth I was declared a heretic. Lord Summerville's plot to assassinate her was discovered and he was executed. Mary, Queen of Scots was also implicated in the conspiracy and was beheaded.

Queen Elizabeth I ordered Sir Francis Drake to attack Vigo and Santo Domingo. The first English colony was established in Newfoundland. England also claimed the West Indies colonies. London's first waterworks were founded, and the first known life insurance. Hideyoshi set up a dictatorship in Japan.

Past (1822-1852)

In USA the religion of Mormons, or Church of Jesus Christ of Latter-day Saints was founded by Joseph Smith in 1830. Like Mohammed before him, he also claimed to have witnessed a vision where an angel revealed to him the Book of Mormon doctrine.

During this Aries Mass Movement many liberal constitutions were implemented around the world. For the first time the word "socialism" came into use in English and French. Charles Dickens published his novels about social injustice in England. Marx and Angels published "The Communist Manifesto."

In addition, the violent Spanish Inquisition that began in the 13th century was finally suppressed. At the same time, the planet of compassion, vision, and ideology, Neptune was discovered (1846).

Many countries became independent republics: Greece, Serbia, Mexico and Cuba. Many Spanish colonies in South America gained independence from Spain: Brazil, Bolivia, Uruguay, Venezuela, Guatemala, Panama, Peru and Santo Domingo. Many U.S. States became autonomous: Texas, Iowa and California. The southern States also began to push for independence from the Union, which led to the devastating Civil War.

Note: Aries Mass movements are primarily about freedom, personal survival and self-interests. The urge for independence becomes uncontrollable; too strong to ignore. When Pluto empowers the pioneering fighting spirit of Aries, actions speak louder than words. If this energy is not directed constructively towards a definite worthy cause, it can turn into anarchy.

Future (2066-2096)

A new independent religion could evolve out of the ashes of the old ones. The new religion will be based on personal responsibility and logic, similar to Buddhism, which started in the 500's B.C. during the previous Aries Age.

During this Mass Movement, people will no longer tolerate any type of suppressive regime. They will pioneer sophisticated systems that will encourage physical fitness, independent thinking, personal initiative and experience.

By this time tyrants will have a difficult time recruiting submissive troops, or blind followers, as people will be more self-assured and better informed.

The Aries Generation (2066-2096)

This Aries Mass Movement will produce a generation of pioneers, soldiers, and driven spiritual warriors, who will rush in where angels fear to tread. Most of them will charge forth heroically for justice, liberty and independence. Others will create turmoil and leave a trail of destruction behind. Most likely, someone from this generation will come forth with the claim of a vision for a new religion, following the lead of a long line of predecessors:

Nostradamus wrote his prophetic quatrains from his visions, the Jewish prophets supposedly wrote the Gospels from their visions, Emperor Constantine created a mighty new empire of Christendom from a vision, Mohammed created the powerful religion of Islam from a vision, and Joseph Smith created the Mormon religion also from a vision. Many Evangelical preachers in America built multi-million religious empires following their "visions."

Visions and dreams have been a common occurrence during this Pisces Age of illusion. Many blind-believers have been fooled and mislead into multiple labyrinths of fantasy. Hopefully, by the time this Aries generation makes its mark upon the world, people will be more aware of paying heed to the Cosmic Law of Cause and Effect (Karma) – for every action there is an equal and opposite reaction.

Cycles of Pluto in Taurus

Keywords

Dependable, Determined, Stable, Persistent, Consistent, Sustaining, Constructive, Patient, Nature, Natural Talents and Abilities.

Ruler: Venus

Resources, Assets, Values, Appreciation, Care, Pleasure, Comfort, Sensual, Creative, Crafty.

Past (1362-1395)

During this Taurus Mass Movement the Aztecs of Mexico built their capital, Tenochtitlan, China restored the Great Wall, Paris built the Bastille, and France coined the first francs. Gothic cathedrals were built throughout Europe and the early Renaissance period began.

Past (1606-1639)

During this Taurus Mass Movement, the first Copper coins were in use. Banks, shops and companies were incorporated.

The island of Manhattan was bought from the Indians for $24.00. The finest of Moslem Mogul architecture, the Taj Mahal of India was built.

Past (1851-1883)

This Taurus cycle brought the unification of Italy as a nation. The new independent nations of the world were establishing their new infrastructure. The U.S. Postal Service was established. The Civil War provided the necessity for the reconstruction process of the American states. The success of holding the Union intact and abolishing slavery transformed American values forever. At the same time, Charles Darwin published "The Origin of the Species."

This cycle marked the onset of the Industrial Revolution. Bridges were being built everywhere, including the Brooklyn Bridge in New York. The first skyscraper was built in Chicago (10 stories) after the Great Fire in 1871.

This Mass Movement also infused the Taurus dogmatic inclinations: The first Vatican Council promulgated the dogma of papal infallibility and the Immaculate Conception of the Virgin Mary.

The American Evangelical alliance and the Ku Klux Klan were founded, and "In God We Trust" first appeared on U.S. coins. The Republican Party was also formed at this time.

The Taurus Generation (1851-1883)

This Taurus Movement gave birth to a generation of future world leaders and U.S. Presidents, among them: Churchill,

Mussolini, Hitler, Teddy Roosevelt, Warren Harding, Calvin Coolidge and Herbert Hoover (President Hoover was partly responsible for the Great Depression of 1930).

This Taurus cycle also produced many self-made multi-millionaires, industrialists, philanthropists, and entrepreneurs, who built the business empires and family dynasties of the new evolving materialistic American culture.

Among them: Rockefeller, Carnegie, Vanderbilt, Dupont, Biltmore, Mellon, Hearst, Woolworth, Hunt, Post, Pulitzer, Hopkins, McCormick, Sears, J.P. Getty, J.P. Morgan, Tiffany, Flagler, Ford. There were many other Hollywood magnates, who established the most successful and powerful movie studios in the history of the world.

Note: As Pluto empowers the old values and corporate empires, stability is severely tested. The entire corporate establishment and financial institutions get uprooted and overhauled. New business empires emerge out of the ashes of the old. The key is to be willing to let go of what has become dysfunctional and obsolete, and hold on to what still has value and purpose.

The Taurus Mass Movements promote building new reliable foundations in anticipation to the new family dynasties that will take the lead during future Cancer Mass Movements.

Furthermore, this cycle prepares the necessary and adequate structures for a multiplicity of new and exciting educational developments associated with the Gemini Mass Movement, which always follows.

Future (2095-2128)

This Taurus Mass Movement will mark a time for recon-struction of the infrastructure and values of the new nations, communities and industries. It will include the use of new currencies, new banking systems, new ways of dealing with international markets, new worldwide manufacturing and environmental laws.

The Taurus Generation (2095-2128)

This Taurus Mass Movement will produce a generation of determined leaders and capable entrepreneurs, who will es-tablish dependable substances that will endure the tests of time.

Cycles of Pluto in Gemini

Keywords

Education, Communication, Transportation, Discernment, Knowledge, Inquisitiveness, Adaptability, Congeniality, Dexterity, Duality.

Ruler: Mercury

Rational, Logical, Clever, Eloquent, Astute, Perceptive, Flexible, Versatile, Vicarious, Restless, Verbose, Changeable.

Past (1395-1425)

This Gemini Mass Movement brought the union of Kalmar between Sweden, Denmark, and Norway. Foreigners in England were forbidden to retail goods. Italy began a revival of Greek literature; they had Greek classes in Florence. A compilation of *Yung Lo Ta Tien Chinese Encyclopedia* in 22,937 volumes was done (only three copies made). *Bellifortis*, book of military technology was written. German refugees from Prague founded the Leipzig University, and St. Andrews University was founded in Edinburgh.

This Gemini Mass Movement gave birth to Johann Gutenberg, future inventor of printing in Europe, and to future Austrian mathematician and astronomer, George Purbach.

Past (1638-1670)

During this Gemini Mass Movement The Peace of Westphalia ended Europe's last great religious war of 30 years. The great Galileo, after having invented the telescope astonished the world with his amazing astronomical discoveries. The Roman Church authorities forced him to deny his scientific discoveries and take a poison. This Gemini cycle gave birth to another scientific giant, Isaac Newton. His revolutionary scientific formulations still remain undisputed by modern academe. The English astrologer William Lilly became famous by his predictions and published books still in use today by astrologers around the world.

Past (1882-1913)

Due to the versatility and mental dexterity of the Gemini Mass Movement, there was an intellectual explosion of literary visionaries and scientific geniuses. Their magnificent achievements and contributions left indelible marks that forever changed the course of history. Among them: Einstein, Edison, Graham Bell, Emerson, Thoreau, Eastman, Ford, Freud, Young, Twain, Darwin, Picasso, Van Gogh, Monet, Lenin, Stalin, Mao Tse-Tung, Marx, H. G. Wells, Oscar Wilde, Bernard Shaw, Thomas Mann, Irving Berlin, Gandhi, and Edgar Casey "the sleeping prophet," who communicated phenomenal words of wisdom while asleep. He made predictions and prescribed remedies for people around the world while his stenographer secretary recorded every word.

The Industrial Revolution brought out many innovative discoveries: psychopathology, theory of relativity, electromagnetic wave, radio, phonograph, telegraph, telephone, electric lamp, locomotive, fluoroscope, improved motion picture cameras, projectors, electrocardiograph, transmission of photographs, automobile batteries, theory of radioactivity, neon lights, fountain pens, and many medical innovations.

Furthermore, in accordance to Gemini's rulership over transportation and siblings, Ford constructed the first Model T and motorbuses, and the brothers Orville and Wilbur Wright built and flew a powered airplane.

The Gemini Generation (1882-1913)

This Gemini Movement gave birth to another generation of multi-talented and intelligent people like Walt Disney and Franklin D. Roosevelt, who later provided their amazing contributions to society during the Leo Mass Movement (1938-58).

Future (2127-2159)

The next Gemini Mass Movement promises to be even greater than the last, as it should be. We can anticipate phenomenal linguistic, literary, and scientific contributions from the geniuses of the previous generations of Aquarius (2033-43) and Pisces (2043-67). Their innate knowledge and wisdom will be disseminated throughout the world. Their accomplishments will make new history for centuries to come, especially in the fields of space communications and exploration, technology and education.

They will apply innovated ideas towards solving the problems of mass transportation, roads, vehicles, and community development. The emphasis on knowledge will encourage the implementation of new school systems and advanced curriculums. Astrology will start to be considered as an integral part of academe.

The Gemini Generation (2127-2159)

This Gemini Mass Movement will produce a new generation of dynamic intellectuals, whose future contributions are unimaginable at the present scope of vision. Among those born at this time will be the long-awaited avatar of the New Aquarius Age (refer to Astronomical Facts in the Aquarius Cycles).

Cycles of Pluto in Cancer

Keywords

Family, Home, Roots, Country, Habits, Tradition, Attachment, Domestic, Defensive, Personal, Tenacious, Patriotic, Ownership.

Ruler: Moon

Maternal, Emotional, Instinctual, Moody, Sensitive, Protective, Retentive, Reflective, Feminine Principle.

Past (1423-1448)

During this Cancer Mass Movement Joan of Arc led the French armies against England, raised siege of Orleans, was captured and burned at the stake at Rouen.

The double-eagle became the emblem of the Holy Roman emperors. Philip of Burgundy created the Order of the Golden Fleece. Heirs to the French throne received the title "Conte du Dauphine." Navigators found the first Negroes near Cape Blanc, western Africa and resumed slave trade.

59

Past (1668-1694)

During this Cancer Mass Movement American territories were opened to people in search of a homestead. New settlements began to spread across the country. While Native Americans were killed for their homelands, African blacks were being snatched from their homes and families to be transported to the Americas at the peak of the slave trade.

In 1692 the witch-hunt hysteria swept through Salem, Massachusetts. Women accused of witchcraft were executed or jailed. Reverend Samuel Parris accused more than 400 women of being allied with the devil in a plot to destroy the Church of Christ in New England. Puritan towns' authorities attributed every natural disaster, loss of livestock, and strange illnesses to women, calling them "witches."

Past (1912-1939)

During this Cancer Mass Movement American women finally won the right to vote after a long struggle. USA experienced a boom in the '20s fuelled by the mass production of automobiles, washing machines, vacuum cleaners, and all the newly available electrical appliances. The American consumer society was born and the nation began its role as a world leader.

America's image of "one big family," "the melting pot," "Mom and apple pie" was established. Owning a home became the indispensable American dream.

The industrial boom attracted emigrants from around the world in search of a better life and a place to raise families. Different nationalities became proud American citizens while retaining their own ethnic identities and traditions. Employers and employees considered themselves part of a family unit, and workers unions began.

However, the dramatically upward spiral of the U.S. stock market ended abruptly in 1929. The first conjunction of Pluto to America's natal Cancer Sun, which caused the rise in economic power, was ultimately responsible for the worst economic depression of the century. Interesting enough, these events coincided with the discovery of Pluto (1930).

The Cancer Generation (1912-1939)

This Cancer Mass Movement gave birth to a large generation of true patriots, who were born during wartime and also participated in most of the wars: the bloody Communist Revolution in "Mother Russia" ended imperial rule, the British occupation of Iraq ended 400 years of Ottoman dominance followed by an armed uprising that restored Arab rule, Spain Civil War, WWI, WWII, Korea, and Vietnam. The WWII group is called, "the greatest generation" in recognition for their bravery and patriotism.

Women also played a critical part in WWII. For the first time, women across the world were no longer forced into the roles society had created for them. They started taking over traditionally male responsibilities: drivers, farmers, garbage collectors, mail delivery, builders, mechanics, factory workers, etc. It became a symbol of freedom and with the increase of freedom, also came an increase of equality.

Many women joined the WAC (Army), WAVE (Navy), and the WASP (Airforce). "Rosie the Riveter" war posters were created, which became an integral part of wartime communi-

61

cation. The posters were designed to instill patriotism, confidence, assist the military, and persuade all Americans to help with the war effort. The posters linked the home front with the military front. This Cancer generation later gave birth to the Leo generation of "baby boomers"—also born during wartime, and grew up to participate in the devastating Vietnam War.

This Cancer Mass Movement also produced the largest group of future women Prime Ministers in the history of the world. Among them: Endira Gandhi, Golda Maier, Margaret Thatcher, Isabel Peron, Corazon Aquino, Soong Ching-Ling.

The women of this Cancer generation made unprecedented strides towards women's rights. Their enormous contributions are evident into the new millennium and have forever changed the tides of time for the women of the world.

Future Cancer Cycle (2518-)

At this particular juncture, and judging from previous Cancer cycles, we can anticipate the same issues to resurface again: nationalism, patriotism, real-estate ownership, family, domestic and women's issues.

By this time, humanity's level of awareness will have improved hence devastating wars will be avoided. Having a Woman President could help in these matters.

Readers are free to extend their imaginations into other distant futures. With logic and reason the pictures will emerge by simply gazing into the past cycles, then applying basic astrological archetypes at a futuristic level.

Cycles of Pluto in Leo

Keywords

Expression, Significance, Dominion, Show, Entertainment, Lavishness, Regal, Dictatorial, Imperial, Dynasty.

Ruler: Sun

Vitality, Drive, Will, Ego, Character, Pride, Honor, Performance, Purpose, Self Identity.

Past (1201-1220)

During this Leo Mass Movement the Roman Christian Crusaders took over Constantinople and established a Latin Empire. Decretal "Venerabilem" asserted superiority of papacy over the empire.

Emperor Michael set up the independent Greek kingdom of Epirus. Theodore Lascaris founded the empire of Nicaea. Otto IV was crowned emperor in Rome and was excommunicated by Pope Innocent III a year later. Francis of Assisi issued the first rules of his brotherhood (the Franciscans). Frederick II was elected German king and made Bohemia a hereditary kingdom.

Official tolerance of European Jews was suspended (1215), as a council convened by Pope Innocent III recognized the existence of "one universal church." No one outside the Catholic Church would be saved. New laws required Jews to be banned from public office and wear specific garments—a precursor to the yellow armbands of Nazi Germany.

Passion plays were among the most dramatic illustrations of the medieval Christian demonization of the Jews. Focusing on the suffering, death, and resurrection of Jesus, performances typically sent many Jews into hiding to avoid mob violence that included ran-sacking their homes and killing them.

Past (1445-1466)

This Leo Mass Movement marked the fall of Constantinople, as well as the onset of the classical culture associated with the European Renaissance. It was a time of great revival in art, literature and learning, initiating the transition from the medieval to the modern world.

At this time Turks captured Constantinople, killed Emperor Constantine and ended the Byzantine Empire. They converted St. Sophia Basilica into a mosque. Turks also conquered Bosnia in the Balkans.

This Leo Mass Movement gave birth to Leonardo da Vinci, Italian Renaissance artist, musician, engineer, and natural scientist. Among his great works: The Last Supper and The Mona Lisa. This Leo cycle also gave birth to Italian navigators Christopher Columbus and Amerigo Vespucci, the great discoverers of the new world.

Past (1692-1712)

This Leo Mass Movement brought the height and fall of the Renaissance "golden age" that started in the previous Leo cycle. This time also witnessed the pinnacle of imperialism. Royalty had self-declared to possess "divine rights," or "in grace." All the kingdoms of the world were competing against each other for supremacy at the time.

Imperial troops were sent around the world in search of new conquests. Gold and other precious commodities were sought regardless of how many lives were destroyed in the process. Many Native Indian Nations were decimated throughout the Americas and the Caribbean. The gold rush began in earnest throughout the new world.

Past (1938-1958)

This Leo Mass Movement brought the rise and fall of egocentric leaders and dictators who had become larger than life: Stalin, Churchill, Hitler, Mussolini, Hirohito, Batista and Fidel Castro. Everything was done in a bombastic way: the holocaust, attack on Pearl Harbor, McCarthyism, U.S. atomic bombs in Hiroshima and Nagasaki, and the Cuban revolution.

During a Leo Mass Movement the drive for significance becomes a contest that goes to extremes. With Leo the term "will live in infamy" (F. D. Roosevelt) takes on a whole new meaning. The world will never forget the millions of war casualties, especially as a result of the atomic bombs.

Furthermore, it is impossible to forget the genocide of millions of Jews in the holocaust. The German dictator Adolph

Hitler tried to eliminate an entire race of people in his egotistical quest for dominance. To the Christian Germans, Hitler became the Christ figure, "the one sent by God" to destroy Judaism and the Jews—not unlike the claim previously made by the Roman Catholic Church about Jesus.

The dramatic side of Leo was also evident in the glorification of WWII and its connection to Hollywood. Movie stars, big bands and performers initiated the trend of entertaining U.S. troops. War was filmed and shown in movie theaters. It was the pinnacle of Hollywood glamour and stardom, and television became a part of every household.

Walt Disney became famous for his creations of animated cartoons and his amusement park "Disneyland." Color cinema on the big screen became extravagant artistic creations. The entertainment business flourished and a whole new renaissance period emerged.

After the war, the Hollywood exuberance subsided with the rise of the McCarthyist furor in America. The right-wing congressman Joseph McCarthy initiated a dictatorship-like, anti-Communist crusade intended to rid the country from the threat of Communism. "McCarthyism" became the witch-hunt of the 20th century.

The anti-communist network was backed by FBI agents and the Supreme Court, and was initially funded by Alfred Kohlberg and the Catholic Church. They imposed a "blacklist" that extended far beyond the Communist party to encompass every liberal in every known industry, especially in show business, including screenwriters and journalists. After the congressional committees had run out of more glamorous targets they turned to the nation's colleges and universities.

They issued Economic Sanctions on businesses accused of fostering communists. Thousands of jobs were lost and careers were destroyed. American citizens, Julius and Ethel Rosenberg became the latest Jewish casualties when they were accused of treason and executed (1951-53).

Public hearings were conducted involving famous Hollywood actors. They were required to publish articles in fan magazines confessing how the party had duped them. Even those who had no party ties had to write a few drafts of their letters until they showed the appropriate degree of contrition. Those who would not, or could not clear themselves became ostracized.

The Leo Generation (1938-1958)

This Leo Mass Movement gave birth to the "baby boomers," or "Me" generation, whose enthusiasm and endless creativity continues to exert a dramatic influence in the 21st century. Besides their significant contributions in leadership and the creative arts, they are credited with the most advanced youth preservation methods and self- improvement tactics in history. They created a whole new industry of self-help books with related products and gadgets. Leo's natural abilities for creating, promoting and marketing lived up to its grandiose expectations.

Due to Leo's adherence to greatness and showmanship, this group is also responsible for creating the new mega-churches with state of the art electronics and Broadway-like productions. They are also responsible for re-creating the lucrative "lecturing circuit" business. Glorified "inspirational speakers" and lecturers in every field became a sensation.

In the "Gay '70s" during the Libra Mass Movement, this Leo group created the trend of "make love, not war," "free love" and self-gratification. It led to an outbreak of venereal diseases in the '80s (Scorpio), followed by the corporate imperialism and superficiality through the '90s and 2000s (Sagittarius). In the '90s the term "yuppie" became the signature definition assigned to this Leo generation.

This group also produced another boom of spoiled children growing up in the Dot/Com Bull markets of the '90s. Leo's insatiable appetite for the good life is reminiscent of the gorging orgies during the pinnacle of the Roman Empire. Similar trends are reflected in the present extravagant lifestyles and depletion of natural resources. Numerous Corporate Empires have been collapsing drastically in the new millennium, as a result of the new kings' (CEO's) unethical illegal practices, egocentricities and overindulgences.

This Leo generation will begin to make their final impact upon the world as they contemplate retirement during the next Capricorn Mass Movement (2008-24). Many of them will avoid retirement altogether, so long as they can continue to exert influential power upon society. Most of them won't settle for anything less than a long and healthy retirement full of fun, leisure and luxury. Others might not be so lucky and are doomed for a rude awakening.

After the imperialistic practices during the Sagittarius and Capricorn movements, there will be no guarantee for a comfortable retirement. The social security fund and other social programs might no longer exist. At this point in time, only the privileged few will be able to enjoy the pleasures of a good life; very similar to the old imperial kingdoms of the past.

Cycles of Pluto in Virgo

Keywords

Service, Organization, Labor, Health, Duty, Commerce, Dedicated, Reliable, Critical, Classifying, Meticulous, Perfectionist.

Ruler: Mercury

Analytical, Literal, Pragmatic, Efficient, Calculating, Technical, Skeptical, Studious.

Past (1218-1233)

During this Virgo Mass Movement tiles replaced thatched and wooden roofs of London houses. Newgate Prison was built in London. Denneborg, the oldest national flag in the world was adopted by Denmark. Vienna became a city.

The Salamanca University, the Naples University and the Toulouse University were founded. The Inquisition in Toulouse began to forbid Bible reading by all laymen. The Christian Crusaders imported the leprosy epidemic to Europe. Coal was minded for the first time in Newcastle, England.

Past (1464-1479)

Monte di Pieta at Orvieto: money loaned at low interest to poor people. The First French printing press was set up in Paris. The French royal mail service was established. Copenhagen University was founded. Dante's "Divine Comedy" was first printed. The First music and the first German Bible were printed. The king and queen of Spain, Ferdinand and Isabella appointed inquisitors against heresy among converted Jews.

Past (1710-1725)

During this Mass Movement, the first national hospitals, libraries and banks opened. England issued the first bank notes, as commercial and slave trade expanded, due to the myriad of colonies being acquired in the Americas, West Indies, East India and other places. The Treaty of Utrecht dismembered the Spanish Empire.

Past (1957-1972)

This Virgo Mass Movement marked the beginning of the Space Program. The Soviet Union launched Sputnik into orbit. In America it was "one giant step for mankind" symbolized by the Moon landing. This cycle also marked the beginning of ecological awareness. Pollution and mind-altering drugs led to deterioration in health of humans, earth, and extinction of many animal species. Many industries had been using America's waterways for dumping deadly contaminants. The environmental disaster prompted the authorities to take pro-active measures in enforcing new laws against pollution. In addition, a very extensive project to clean out lakes and rivers was initiated, which eventually produced positive results.

The Soviet Union invaded Czechoslovakia and Germany erected the Berlin wall. The Cuban Missiles Crisis in 1962, a confrontation between the US and USSR was a frightening experience. It demonstrated to the world the grim threat of nuclear war. Fear ultimately helped to convince the two nations of the need for less "cold war" tactics and more dialogue and negotiations.

The civil rights movement erupted with violent demonstrations and riots. Top leaders and supporters of human rights were murdered including the peaceful leader Rev. Martin L. King, the US President John F. Kennedy and his brother Robert. Thus, African-Americans were finally granted civil rights, allowed to vote, and the public school system became integrated.

The controversial and devastating Vietnam War was in progress and demonstrations against it grew larger around the country. Government officials ordered the U.S. National Guard to forcefully restrain university students from dissenting. American intervention ended up withdrawing, as the North Vietnamese forces prevailed. The longest war in U.S. history caused 56,000 American lives and more than $141 billion in war expenditures. Vietnamese casualties were estimated at 1.3 million lives.

The Virgo Generation (1957-1972)

This Virgo Mass Movement gave birth to a generation of concerned citizens, activists, political and religious followers, due to Virgo's affinity for order and discrimination.

Many of this generation are the environmentalists of the 21st century, who are protesting the World Bank and World Trade organizations that refuse to be accountable for the exploitation of workers, the poor and the planet.

This Virgo generation has been called "the Tweeners" because they are caught between "Boomers" and "Xers." These are the computer wiz's, the dedicated faithful workers and soldiers, who are holding up the fort in the new millennium. Most of them struggle between unemployment, low-paying jobs and no health insurance. Many professionals with college degrees have been forced to accept menial jobs, while others have joined the Armed Forces to earn a living.

In this cycle Pluto magnifies Virgo's propensity to be "caught between a rock and a hard place," and to "miss the forest for the trees," due to intense concentration on details. The challenge is self-adjustments leading to self-reliance.

In the new millennium, this group has been the most directly affected by the collapses of conglomerate corporate empires, as well as corporate cost reductions and massive layoffs.

Virgo's main concerns include basic civil rights, education, decent jobs and health care. This is precisely where deficiencies are reaching dangerous proportions. To make matters worse, conservative lawmakers have been dismantling the Labor Unions that used to protect the interests of average workers.

This Virgo generation will continue to act as catalysts for justice and equality among the working people. Some of them will continue working diligently for churches, the Arm Forces, Homeland Security, schools, hospitals, and other community services.

Many of them will continue to promote the reorganization and cleansing of corrupt government and religious systems throughout the present Sagittarius Movement, and thereafter into the Capricorn Movement (2008-2024).

This particular group will remain specifically involved in the health-care crisis, national security crisis, and financial collapse caused by the imperialistic practices of their predecessors the Leo generation, alias "Baby Boomers."

The Virgo generations always have to end up cleaning the mess left by their exuberant predecessors. After Leo takes it all, Virgo is forced to reorganize and start all over again from scratch. It is part of their destiny and Virgos are perfectly capable of accomplishing the job.

Cycles of Pluto in Libra

Keywords

Partnerships, Legalities, Contracts, Culture, Art, Balance, Mediation, Ethics, Treaties.

Ruler: Venus

Love, Grace, Romance, Charm, Harmony, Beauty, Sharing, Mating, Sociable, Diplomatic.

Past (1232-1244)

During this Libra Mass Movement the Pope entrusted the Dominicans with the Inquisition. The Arabs lost Cordoba to Castile (Spanish kingdom). The Mongols conquered Russia. A border was fixed between England and Scotland. A five-year truce was arranged between England and France. Italian poet Guido Guinizelli established a school of poetry.

Past (1478-1491)

This Mass Movement brought the union of Aragon and Castile under Ferdinand the Catholic and Isabella. They financed the first voyage of Christopher Columbus to the new world (1492). They also initiated the Spanish Inquisition under the joint direction of State and Church. The Spanish Empire consolidated and aimed at regaining their original culture after extinguishing the Moorish kingdom throughout Spain. It took Spain another complete cycle of Pluto to finish the process.

Past (1724-1737)

During this Libra cycle Spain fully recovered their original culture after a long process of elimination. Anyone left with an ounce of Moorish blood was killed or expelled. Many new treaties and alliances between empires and countries were made. Many new cultures began to emerge, especially the new American culture, as the new colony was expanding. The American Freemason Lodge was founded. The cultural icon, Benjamin Franklin issued *Poor Richard's Almanac*.

Past (1971-1984)

This Libra Mass Movement launched the women's liberation movement. As a result, a whole new colorful and original culture emerged. The Libra aesthetic qualities were reflected in the psychedelic fashions and "disco" music. The "Go-Go" dancers became a sensation.

Mainly single women dependent on the system for support were raising children. The Libra influence also led to the onset of the multi-million dollar stripping and porno industry. It was altogether a sexual revolution. Uninhibited and unrestricted love was the ultimate purpose.

During this cycle Indira Gandhi was elected Prime Minister of India, Margaret Thatcher became Prime Minister of England, and Maria Pintassilgo became Portugal's Prime Minister.

TV talk shows discussing personal relationships and social problems became popular. For the first time a government trial was televised. The trial of the "Watergate" break-ins perpetrated by government officials overwhelmed the country. Americans watched their trusted government officials being prosecuted for burglary and other illegalities, inclusive of the U.S. President, who was forced to resign for conspiracy. It was a cultural shock to the nation from which, it may never fully recover.

In addition, Egypt and Syria initiated a failed war against Israel. The U.S. President arranged a Mideast Peace summit followed by the drafting of a bilateral peace treaty by officials from Israel and Egypt in Washington D.C. An unstable ceasefire has remained in force with U.S. involvement in between Arabs and Israelis that continues unresolved.

The European Parliament was elected. In Chile a military junta overthrew the Marxist President. In Argentina, Juan Peron and his wife were elected President and Vice President. Many Central American nations were in upheaval, as leftist guerrillas struggled to overthrow the old oppressive regimes. South Africa was also in turmoil to end the apartheid.

China and USA announced the establishment of full diplomatic relations. The U.S. President and Panama's chief of government signed the new Panama Canal treaties. The Bahamas were granted independence from Britain after three centuries of partnership with colonial rule.

In Iran, the Shah (Persian for king) was forced into exile. The fundamentalist Islamic regime of Ajatollah Khomeini replaced the old traditional constitutional monarchy. Similar circumstances occurred in Iraq with the rise and rule of Saddam Hussein, whose ruthless regime rose to power after executing the sitting king.

The most classic example of a Libra cycle was the mass murder/suicide in November 1978 of the Jonestown cult in the South American republic of Guyana. Jim Jones, the self proclaimed prophet, led about 1000 of his loyal followers to their death. At the time, he was under investigation by the U.S. authorities for illegal activities.

Cults and "communes" became very popular during this Libra cycle. Many young people were lured into abandoning their homes and families to join divertive cults and live in communes as one big family. They shared possessions, sex partners, children and drugs. This trend came to a halt after the deplorable "Manson family" criminal case. Many parents hired professional help to find their kids and have them deprogrammed.

This Libra Mass Movement also brought about the infamous "swingers' clubs" for married couples seeking excitement and variety. The divorce rate increased to unprecedented levels.

The Libra Generation (1971-1984)

This Libra Movement gave birth to the so-called "generation X," who experienced disintegration of the marital institution. Most of these children grew up relying more on their piers than on their own parents. They are the team players and

78

groupies, who favor friends and piers from their relatives.

This Libra generation produced many original artists such as, "brake dancers" and "Rappers." They share their stories through their music, while exposing the social dysfunctions of society. They are also known by their tattoos, body piercing, group dancing and performing, and for the "mush pit" (diving onto the crowd at concerts).

Although this Libra generation is highly competitive, their main concern is peace and companionship. These are the faithful troops of the world, who are ready to do whatever it takes to defend their particular culture, sect, team, or group. Ironically, in the quest for peace sometimes it takes war to achieve. This group is perfectly suited for the military. Thus, where this group is concerned, it is not a matter of patriotism. Since their personal identity is related to their counterparts, what really matters to them the most is team fidelity.

The particular influence of the Libra generation is most evident on the new millennial television programs, where they are divided into teams while diplomatically plotting to outsmart and outdo the others.

Many in this generation could become future cult leaders. Others will become diplomats, social directors, artists and legal counselors. They will strive to achieve balance between incongruous forces and eventually will act as catalysts to reform the legal system. Social laws were already changed on their account; children who commit grave crimes are now treated as adults thus sentenced accordingly.

This Libra generation will strive to protect women's reproductive rights and legalize gay marriages. Libra has no gender priorities; their motto is reconciliation and unification through objectivity. Thus, as soon as this generation is ready to take charge, they will undoubtedly make drastic changes regarding traditional ritualistic religious services.

Already, many Christian churches have adopted popular music, concerts and youth clubs in order to attract and accommodate this particularly gregarious Libra generation. This group will eventually turn religious churches into secular organizations for the primary purpose of communal social events.

This Libra generation will also be left with the task of repairing the international relationships that are being damaged during the Sagittarius and Capricorn Movements. Most importantly, it is impendent upon them to bring about final resolutions to the Middle East conflict—once and for all, one way or another.

The intellectual and social consciousness side of Libra is very compatible with the Aquarius energy. Thus, as it is to be expected, this Libra generation will be ready to make a dynamic impact upon the world during the next Aquarius Mass Movement (2023-43).

Cycles of Pluto in Scorpio

Keywords

Crime, Sex, Tax, Death, Legacies, Mystery, Suspicion, Investigation, Espionage, Research, Manipulation, Transformation, Healing.

Ruler: Pluto

Power, Control, Desire, Obsessive, Possessive, Compulsive, Underhanded, Intrigue, Secrets, Psychoanalysis, Probe, Destruction, Rebirth.

Past (1243-1256)

During this Scorpio Movement the Egyptian Khwarazmi took over Jerusalem. Frederick II seized the vacant dukedom of Austria and Styria. The Seventh Crusade, led by Louis IX landed in Egypt and the Saracens captured him. Moslems began work on the Alhambra in Granada, Spain. It became the most elaborate sumptuous palace of the Moorish kingdom as a symbol of power over the conquest of Spain. Later, during the Spanish Inquisition, the King of Spain took over the palace and made it his home.

At this time the Inquisition began to use instruments of torture. In Spain they chained infidels (Jews and Moslems) to the outside walls of Christian churches while people spit at them and stoned them.

Past (1490-1503)

During this Mass Movement papal bull Erasmus ordered the burning of books thought to be against the authority of the Church. Crimes against humanity were rampant at the pinnacle of the Inquisition. People accused of heresy were burned at the stake. The massive deaths prompted the need to open the first European orphanages. The Syphilis epidemic spread from Italy throughout Europe.

This Scorpio Mass Movement gave birth to future Italian politician Niccolo Machiavelli (1469-1527). He was to become famous by advocating the need of a ruler to enhance and preserve his power by whatever means necessary.

Past (1736-1749)

During this Scorpio Mass Movement piracy on the high seas was rampant. England implemented new taxes and Scotland abolished hereditary jurisdiction.

European monarchies were in upheaval during the Protestant Reformation Movement. People were being persecuted and killed for political and religious reasons. In England the Whigamores were opposed to the power of the Crown. There was conspiracy, intrigue and violence.

Past (1983-1995)

This Scorpio cycle was at the peak of the Cold War. There were abundant power games, international spies and intrigue. Power struggles and corruption was evident in governments. The U.S. President called the Soviet Union "the evil empire."

In early '80s, USA was secretly involved in supporting the Taliban in Afghanistan against Russia, and Iraq against Iran. There were political wars in Panama, Granada and Iraq.

The Iran-Contra scandal implicated the CIA and Republican Administration of trading arms for hostages and other covert schemes. They were selling illegal arms and using the money for overthrowing leftwing governments in Central and South America. The purpose was to preserve the old oppressive imperialistic regimes aligned with USA.

U.S. officials ordered the CIA to work closely with corrupt military officers, who were known to moonlight as cocaine traffickers and money-launderers, in building up the contra army. They made deals with the Drug Lords to ignore the smuggling, provided they donated a percent of the drugs' profits to the contra armies.

Meanwhile, the administration kept battling Congress to continue the CIA money flowing. The contra-narcotics operation resulted in the devastating flood of cocaine that swept through U.S. cities with destruction, addiction and violence.

Beyond withholding the evidence, the administration mounted public relations attacks on members of Congress, journalists and witnesses exposing the crimes. CIA operatives claimed the counter-narcotics mission did not have as high a priority, as the missions against communist insurrections in South America. They claimed Cuba was conducting clandestine operations to infiltrate communism into South America. The rise in power of the underworld and Drug Lords led to major deterioration of entire American cities and S. American countries.

During this Scorpio Movement, Israel began "Operation Moses," a secret airlift of Ethiopian Jews (Falashas) from Sudan; 25,000 were airlifted. The Prime Minister of India Indira Gandhi was assassinated by her Sikh bodyguards. Her son Rajicv became the new Prime Minister. Anti-Sikh riots swept India with over 1,000 deaths.

The sins of greed, deviousness, covetousness and jealousy get out of control in a Scorpio cycle. There was financial fraud among powerful people who bankrupted the Savings & Loans banks forcing taxpayers to pick up the tab; it created a significant recession. In addition, a trend of several kingpins in the TV Evangelical Empire collapsed for fraudulent practices and sex scandals.

The President of the Philippines, Ferdinand Marcos was forced to flee the country after alleged ballot rigging. Corazon Aquino became the new President. Haitian President Jean-Claude Duvalier escaped to France after nationwide demonstrations against his imperialistic rule.

This Scorpio cycle brought out an explosion of sexually transmitted diseases and AIDS virus. There were massacres, famine, and genocide in Rwanda, Somalia and Ethiopia. The same was happening in Bosnia and the Balkans in 1991, after Marshall Tito's rule ended and Yugoslavia blew apart.

Hundreds of American soldiers died in Lebanon when Shiite Muslims bombed the American barracks during a bloody war between Israelis and Palestinians. Ten years later during the same Scorpio cycle American troops were defeated in Somalia by Drug Lords who were starving the people and terrorizing the country. The U.S. mission came to a halt after a violent mob dragged the body of an American soldier through the streets of Mogadishu.

As it was to be expected, this Scorpio cycle brought back the occult and gave birth to the New Age Movement. New Age stores and Psychic Fairs swept the country. Palm and Tarot card "fortune-tellers" became popular. Psychics and "channelers" of dead spirits became the latest fad.

One woman in particular became rich and famous impersonating a powerful discarnate male, so-called "master," whom she gave the exotic name of Ramtha. Star-stroke audiences paid hundreds of dollars to attend her performances of pontification and philosophical jargon. She also made a fortune on books and tapes, until her husband exposed her and both ended up in bankruptcy and disgrace. Psychic phone lines also became a very lucrative business, until most of them were found fraudulent.

The occult provides the perfect forum for unqualified people, whose main objective is self-importance, the appearance of power, and financial gain—not unlike religion. Many so-called, "faith healers" of the Christian persuasion are also guilty for exploiting the gullible. The belief in magic that starts in the Scorpio Movement turns into the glorified supernatural in Sagittarius. The similarities are unquestionable.

Just as there are legitimate religious ministers, there are legitimate psychics and legitimate professional astrologers, whose main concern is to provide valuable services to the community. They prefer not to seek the limelight, usually working behind the scenes with the police, psychotherapists, educational organizations, the business sector and the public, helping to transform lives for the better. They are the unpretentious and unselfish metaphysical teachers and spiritual healers of the world.

During this cycle, Iraqi troops led by the dictator Saddam Hussein invaded and ransacked neighboring Kuwait in a futile effort to take possession of the region. This led to U.S. intervention and the Gulf War, Desert Storm.

Positive transformations occurred with the collapse of Communism in the Soviet Union and Eastern Europe. The removal of the Berlin Wall was a major victory. In the USA hurricane Andrew devastated South Florida and the insurance industry.

During this Scorpio cycle, government and religious authorities were persecuting doctor Jack Kevorkian, alias "Dr. Death" and self-described "angel of mercy," for his unrelenting crusade to legalize the practice of euthanasia. After 130 successful assisted suicides by terminally ill patients and a myriad of trials, he was sentenced to prison in April 1999. While physicians across the country often perform the same medical services for the wealthy elite behind the scenes, he was the only one doctor brave enough to be willing to stand up and put his life on it.

From February 28 to April 19, 1993, there was a standoff in Waco, Texas between the FBI, ATF, and the doomed cult of Branch Davidians. Their leader, David Koresh, was a psychotic self-proclaimed "prophet of God." According to a former member, Koresh was prophesying for himself 60 wives,

80 concubines and "virgins without number."

The ATF raid was sparked by the claim of David's sex with girls as young as 12 and his arsenal of paramilitary illegal weapons. The cultists refused to come out and government agents were killed in the shootout. A cult member was seen setting the Mount Carmel compound ablaze where they all perished, including the children.

During this Scorpio cycle, Catholic priests were exposed for sexual molestation of children for the first time in the history of the Church. It was also discovered that church officials had been covering up the scandal for many years. It cost the church millions for the prosecution of the guilty priests.

The President of USA was accused of denying a sexual indiscretion with a female intern. It caused the biggest sex scandal in the history of American politics. His inquisitors published and televised sexually explicit language that shocked the nation and the world. The First Lady accused them of a "right wing conspiracy."

After subjecting the country to a drilling impeachment trial, the charges were not found to be impeachable under the law. The entire fiasco was obviously designed by powerful politicians and their religious cohorts, for the purpose of destroying a popular President, who did not support their particular agenda.

A famous sports hero was accused of murdering his wife and friend, which resulted in the most televised "trial of the century." His powerful team of lawyers ("the dream team") managed to get him acquitted despite all the evidence against him, including DNA.

The Internet brought the economic boom of the '90s. Dot/Com entrepreneur's businesses produced many new millionaires, while trading stocks on line became a profitable vocation. The anonymity provided by the Internet became the perfect outlet for sexual perverts and other criminals who prey on unsuspecting victims. On the other hand, the magical hidden world of the Internet can transform lives for the best. It may well prove to be the greatest learning tool available in the 21st century. The Scorpio issues of investigation, research, financial planning, investments, covert operations, underground activities, and other joint endeavors are what the Internet is all about.

During this Scorpio Mass Movement the "Gothic" dress style was the popular trend among the young. They wore all black clothing, makeup and chain accessories. The most popular movies were about greed, sex and violence. "Greed is Good" became a cliché. Also at this time there were multiple cases of Americans, including FBI agents, with access to classified information that were caught selling secrets to the Russians.

The Scorpio Generation (1983-1989)

This Scorpio Mass Movement gave birth to a generation constantly threatened by death. It produced many "born-killers," such as the ones involved in school shootings throughout the '90s.

Some are attracted to satanic cults in a misguided quest for power. This Scorpio group holds the highest record of teenage suicide in history. Others will do very well as trained soldiers and mercenaries fighting the new wave of terrorism around the world. They are the warriors, perpetrators, and victims as well.

Scorpio also produces superstitious people who can turn into religious fanatics, due to an unconscious fear of divine retribution and loss of control. Many of them will gladly offer their lives in exchange for the promise of a place in heaven or paradise, not unlike the Islamic suicide bombers. Others will simply choose to become career criminals.

The more evolved souls from this generation will become therapists, surgeons, astrologers, clergy, psychics, researchers, forensic scientists, morticians, coroners, funeral directors, mortgage and insurance agents, tax collectors, stockbrokers, law enforcement agents, and investigators in all fields of human endeavor.

They will strive to expose corruption and explore the complexities of hidden mysteries in order to transform darkness into light, and then turn it into healing power for all humanity.

Summary

Life on Planet Earth follows a precise pattern; "To everything there is a season, a time for every purpose under heaven, a time to sow and a time to reap" (Ecclesiastes 3). In God's perfect system evil exists because it is empowered by ignorance. Enlightenment is the only force under the sun capable of destroying evil.

Souls need to learn from their own mistakes, even if it takes a few lifetimes. Awareness of planetary cycles helps to accelerate the evolutionary growth process. Furthermore, learning from history allows humanity to change destiny. Evil would be significantly inhibited in an enlightened world!

The stars reveal the purpose of our existence, inclusive of universal secrets. The scientific evidence presented in this book concerning Pluto's cycle and its effect upon world events, supports the old belief that "everything happens for a reason." The *reason* is always written in the stars. The *purpose* is to create a better future where souls are free to grow and evolve as high as their aspirations and natural capabilities allow them to.

Life on Planet Earth is part of a sophisticated universal spiral system; while spinning on its own axis, it is forever moving outwards and forwards thus stagnation, or backward movement go against the natural forces of the universe with devastating results.

Life is better understood looking backwards, but it must always be lived looking forwards. Thus, everyone is entitled to move forward at his/her own pace. There is perfect order in the universe; the firmament and the heavenly bodies were created for a purpose.

Every living organism on earth, humans included, is impelled by the energy emanating from the cosmos. No one can escape it—it is unavoidable. The human body, most especially the brain, operates on electrical impulses thus is subject to interference much like a radio. But, how we respond to that cosmic energy depends entirely on the individual nature and level of awareness. It is not easy to believe how the energy of a distant small planet like Pluto can produce a mass movement; like a plague that spreads through the collective consciousness, and yet, the evidence is undeniable, if we only take the time to notice.

Astrology is not a belief or superstition, it is a study based on cold, hard facts. This debate has been going on for centuries. Despite the unsubstantiated claims from "debunkers" and naysayers ignorant in the subject, astrology has survived the test of time. It is one of the oldest sciences in the world.

Systematic research into cycles began in the 1920s at Harvard University under the direction of Professor Ellsworth Huntington. The idea that celestial phenomena, repeating according to a set schedule, could predict the course of human affairs here on Earth was not a new one to astrologers, of course. But, Huntington and his research team proved without a doubt that cycles operated in biological, economic, political, and other human fields. As Huntington wrote about the findings, "All this may suggest Astrology…"

Interconnection Between Pluto's Cycle, Mass Movements, and the Zodiacal Signs

The transit of Pluto through the constellations (signs) creates World Mass Movements pertinent to the main purpose of each sign. Due to Pluto's qualities of empowerment and transformation, the rise created is ultimately followed by a fall. This process promotes the need to <u>reassess</u> the issues at hand. Consequently each Mass Movement leads to the next.

Example: After the Pisces Mass Movement (#12) *causes* the rise and fall of blind faith, thus *creating* the need for rectifying victimization and bondage, it naturally *leads* to the quest for *independence* and new beginnings in the Aries Mass Movement (#1).

Beginning with the first sign of the zodiac, the following synopsis clearly depicts the interconnection between World Mass Movements and the signs of the zodiac:

1. Aries. The rise and fall of *independence* create the need for <u>redirecting</u> courage and conviction leads to Taurus.

2. Taurus. The rise and fall of *old structures* create the need for <u>reconstructing</u> the infrastructure and values leads to

95

Gemini.

3. Gemini. The rise and fall of *educational systems* create the need for <u>redistributing</u> information and knowledge leads to Cancer.

4. Cancer. The rise and fall of *tradition and nationalism* create the need for <u>reestablishing</u> foundations leads to Leo.

5. Leo. The rise and fall of *imperial centralization* create the need for <u>recognizing</u> creative self-expression leads to Virgo .

6. Virgo. The rise and fall of the *military industrial complex* create the need for <u>reorganizing</u> labor and civil rights leads to Libra.

7. Libra. The rise and fall of *cultural identity* create the need for <u>rediversifying</u> social standards leads to Scorpio.

8. Scorpio. The rise and fall of *corruption* create the need for <u>reawakening</u> the use of power and control leads to Sagittarius.

9. Sagittarius. The rise and fall of *religion-law-ethnicity* create the need for <u>redefining</u> international relations leads to Capricorn.

10. Capricorn. The rise and fall of *authoritarian administrations* create the need for <u>reevaluating</u> government and corporate power leads to Aquarius.

11. Aquarius. The rise and fall of *revolutionary groups* create the need for <u>reforming</u> the social system leads to Pisces.

12. Pisces. The rise and fall of *blind faith* create the need for <u>rectifying</u> victimization and bondage leads back to Aries.

The above correlations confirm the fact that Divine Intelligence, or Infinite Spirit, set in motion a universe on its own trajectory, an automatic scientific system of cosmic energy and cycles where everything happens accordingly, and on schedule.

We are spiritual beings endowed with free will, living in a well-organized system of evolution thus challenged to combine the scientific with the spiritual—each is incomplete without the other.

Scientists can explain the process of evolution at a physical level, but without recognizing the evolution of the soul they give people no other choice than to blame God for everything: fortunes, misfortunes, and natural catastrophes.

Scientists can explain the physical nature of the heavenly bodies (planets), but fail to recognize their divine influence and purpose. Incomplete science leads to wrong conclusions and distorted justifications hence holding back the evolutionary growth process of humanity.

Acknowledging the perfect union between science and spirituality would put an end to the conflict between creation and evolution. In addition, it would encourage humanity to assume a higher level of self-responsibility—for individual fate, as well as the fate of our magnificent planet.

Pluto's cycle is one among many other meaningful planetary cycles constantly at work in the universe. The interconnection that exists between the heavenly bodies and life here on Earth is not a fantasy—it is a common reality. Planetary cycles prove that history cannot be stopped from repeating, but awareness could make a big difference.

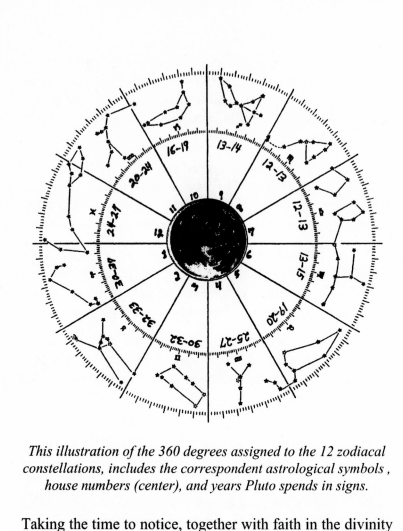

This illustration of the 360 degrees assigned to the 12 zodiacal constellations, includes the correspondent astrological symbols , house numbers (center), and years Pluto spends in signs.

Taking the time to notice, together with faith in the divinity behind the process leads to enlightenment. The right combination of science and spirituality is about providing tools for wise people to use to the fairest advantage for the most, so that comfort, happiness and security will conform to the best in a world of probable outcomes.

In Search of the True Nativity

Was baby Jesus really born the 25th of December? "The Gospel according to Hallmark" says it was. However, if we examine our solid historical sources there is absolutely nothing to suggest that date.

The information presented here is based on my own research and astrological expertise, as well as on the book, *Astrology's Pew in Church*. The author is Reverend Donald J. Jacobs, Ordained Methodist Minister and pastor of 11 Missouri churches. The Reverend's intensive research for the true birth of Jesus led him to become a professional astrologer.

Let us begin with the historical fact that Christmas does not mean Jesus' birthday, but only a mass in honor of the Christ. December 25 was a yearly pagan festival celebrating the time of the universal ancient winter solstice holiday. This happens to be the longest, darkest night of the year. Each year on December 21, the sun enters the sign of Capricorn where it descends into the lowest parts of the earth, as far south as it can go (the tropic of Capricorn).

The sun seems to remain stationary on that same latitude for three days and three nights until midnight of December 24. At this time it rises again (rebirth) from the depths to begin its journey back north. This was one of the highest mass celebrations among the early Christians, as well as the pagans.

Because of the symbolism of resurrection on this particular holiday, and as part of a deliberate campaign to replace the old festivals of the pagan calendar, they chose this date to celebrate the birth of Christ.

The early Christians had another reason for the midnight "Christ Mass" celebration on the 24th; when Jesus the Christ (Christ means anointed) was asked for a sign he said; "no sign will be given it except the sign of the prophet Jonah, for as Jonah was 3 days and 3 nights in the whale's belly (earth), so shall the son of man be 3 days and 3 nights in the heart of the earth," Matthew 12:39:40.

In the Gospel according to Matthew and Luke who are the only ones responsible for the historical mention of Jesus' birth, they both specifically place His birth in the reign of king Herod. Herod died on the lunar eclipse in March of 4 BC. The Bible and archeological records of ancient clay tablets, which show a continuing careful year-long observation of the triple conjunction of Jupiter and Saturn in the sign Pisces in 7 BC, mark the most probable time for the birth of Jesus.

Most scholars agree on this because there had to be, between the Nativity and Herod's death, time for the Magi to travel 1000 miles from Mesopotamia to Jerusalem. This, by Herod's own guess took a year or two. This also gave time for the holy family to flee to Egypt and settle there for a while before Herod died.

The "Blazing Star" being overhead when the child was born is nothing but folklore. The Star of Bethlehem was not noticed by anyone but astrologers.

The Magi (*magoi* in the Greek original, meaning astrologers—the Bible does not say three and does not says kings, it says astrologers), showed up about a year after the manger birth, after the holy family had moved into a house. Matthew says in Gospel 2:11, "And going into the house they saw the child with Mary his mother, and they fell down and worshiped him."

Matthew mentioned no shepherds, angels, or manger. Luke tells of shepherds seeing a vision of angels, but there is no mention of a star, wise men, kings or astrologers because they were not there that night, and in fact, never came to the stable-manger at all.

This is clearly indicated in Matthew's 2:2 (correctly translated in the Revised Standard Version) "Where is he who has been (past tense) born king of the Jews? For we have seen (past tense) his star when we were in the East and have come to worship him."

In 1603, the famous astronomer Johannes Kepler first calculated the triple conjunction of Jupiter and Saturn of 7 BC and suggested that this was the star of Bethlehem. Thus, it took an astrologer to examine the astrological qualifications for the specific birthday of the little Hebrew baby, whose birth stars attracted astrologers across thousands of miles of desert.

For 20 years Rev. Jacobs accumulated and analyzed all the data available on the historical Jesus, in undergraduate Bible school and graduate theological seminary. He even computed the angle of the Jerusalem to Bethlehem road in terms of what time of year the Jupiter-Saturn conjunction would have blinked into view at sunset. His findings indicated that the Magi arrived in early January 6 BC, ten months after the manger birth.

We know that Herod was vicious, but if the wise men were seeking a baby born that day, or to be born that night, it would have been simpler to kill all the new-born infants without including the two year old toddlers. (January 6 is still celebrated in the Roman Catholic Church as "The Epiphany" in honor of "The Three Wise Men").

Since astrologers came all the way from Babylon in response to something they saw in the sky, Rev. Jacobs also researched classical astrology. He found that Gjamasp, the great Persian astrologer of about 500 BC had predicted that when the great conjunction fell in Pisces, a great history-changing prophet would appear among them.

Jupiter and Saturn conjunct every 20 years in different signs, but they don't always make three conjunctions in the same year, which is due to a process called retrograde motion. In addition, about every 240 years the conjunction changes to a different "element." This process is defined as "mutations," which can also happen with any other planetary cycle. However, the particular cycle of Jupiter-Saturn denoted the birth of kings.

This time, Gjamasp had predicted that the Great King of the Hebrews would be born and the Age of Pisces would begin in the next triple mutation into the water Element in Pisces, the sign of the Jewish nation. That is precisely what occurred in 7 BC. The three conjunctions were exact on May 24, October 1, and December 9.

The extremely rare triple conjunction brought the "wise men," but the entire map made Jesus the very special person who personifies the Piscean Age. After studying the position of the planets for the entire year from 7 BC to 6 BC, Reverend Jacobs first concluded that Jesus could not have been born in the winter when the sheep were kept at night in stable caves and not out on the hillsides.

Furthermore, the Jewish Mishnah Laws against cruelty to animals prohibited shepherding on the frigid winter nights of the Judean highlands from December to about March 1. Most importantly, Jesus did not have anything in common with the sign Capricorn. This would make him an excellent businessman, but certainly not a martyr.

Knowing astrology, it was obvious that "the Savior of the new age of Pisces" would have to posses the qualities of the sign Pisces. Pisces people go for self-sacrifice, kindness, tend to be psychic and speak in parables, among other things. Besides, Jesus' followers chose as their symbol a fish referring to their Pisces Savior.

Some modern astronomers have made ridiculous assumptions that Jesus must have been born on the new Moon of April 17, 6 BC. Not only is this date unsubstantiated, it makes Jesus an Aries. This would have made Him an unrelenting leader, soldier, warrior like Moses. Aries is the furthest away from a martyr as anyone can get.

After all these considerations and analysis, Rev. Jacobs finally found the most powerful horoscope he had ever seen. But, in order to ascertain its accuracy, he had to correlate all the events in Jesus life to that horoscope, from birth to crucifixion. He found that it fit Jesus perfectly. The ministry, retreat to Tyre, Crucifixion and even the Resurrection was clearly marked and perfectly timed.

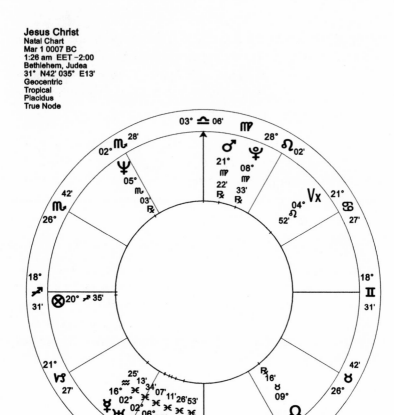

Jesus Christ
Natal Chart
Mar 1 0007 BC
1:26 am EET −2:00
Bethlehem, Judea
31° N42' 035° E13'
Geocentric
Tropical
Placidus
True Node

The date was March 1, 6 BC, at 1: 26 AM, E.U.T. -2, Bethlehem, Judea. It is important to point out that 6 BC comes out as 7 BC because there was never a 0 year.

One glance at the horoscope itself shows that the power of the heavens peak at the particular moment, when the Sun and Moon join Venus, Jupiter and Saturn forming a cluster at the heart of the mystical Pisces in the third house of communication and education.

Mercury, the planet of the mind and the spoken word is in the unconventional and humanitarian sign of Aquarius in the second house of values and resources. Mars, planet of war and aggression is opposing the Pisces cluster from the ninth house of religion and belief systems.

Heavy clusters of planets such as this, is an indication of some type of genius. Pisces is the sign of transcendence, creative inspiration, imagination, and has a need for introspection and withdrawal. According to the Bible, Jesus escaped many times to find solitude in the desert and the hills. It was also very Piscean of Jesus to belong to a mystical secret sect like the "Essenes," who were the astrologers at that time.

This horoscope is even more powerful than it first seemed to the Magi because at the time, there were only seven visible planets including the sun and moon. Uranus, the planet of change and genius, unknown to astrologers of the time makes the sixth planet in the Pisces cluster exactly conjunct Jupiter. This combination shows extreme originality by which to devise totally new philosophical and religious concepts.

The Magi did not see the spiritual planet Neptune either, ruler of Pisces and placed in the eleventh house of humanitarian aspirations, social contribution, and friends. Neptune is making positive trine aspects (ease, gifts, talents) to the Pisces cluster. This particular configuration shows extraordinary, empathetic psychic ability, kindness, and unfathomable spirituality.

Pisces and Neptune also represent betrayal, mystery, defeat, which explains why his friend Judas betrayed him, not for his whereabouts, but for the Messianic secret. As soon as his secret was forced out of him, he was condemned to death.

Secretive Scorpio in the twelfth house of Karma, persecution, self-sacrifice and misfortune also indicates the same. The ruler of Scorpio is Pluto (also unknown then), the powerful planet of death/rebirth (transformation) and violence, is near Mars and making enough oppositions to the Pisces cluster to get anyone crucified on account of his beliefs and ideals (ninth house).

Pluto in the ninth also shows a fanatical sense of Messianic destiny. The Sagittarius ascendant makes him philosophical, truthful, high-minded, freedom loving, and a tendency to dispute authority. The above is only a short interpretation, but there is no doubt this is the horoscope of a truly extraordinary man.

If the Bible were really against astrology, as the negativists fundamentalists claim, imagine the outrage when the astrologers came to Jerusalem seeking for the new king. The Sanhedrin, the Council of Bible scholars who ruled religious Judaism would have stoned the astrologers to death. Instead, they welcomed them as honored guests and respectfully questioned them about the star.

The Sanhedrin correlated this revelation with the prophetic tradition that the Messiah would be born in Bethlehem, and with Numbers 24:17— "A star shall come forth out of Jacob." It was astrology and the Bible working together that finally brought the "wise men" to Jesus, and it was their gifts what financed the holy family's escape into Egypt.

Unfortunately, the same Biblical scholars that welcomed the good news, later on were also responsible for condemning Jesus. They were disappointed, because they expected the Messiah to be a supernatural "angel-of-the-Lord," who would appear in the clouds leading angelic armies. This is remarkably similar to what modern fundamentalists still believe and preach.

The prophet Daniel would be very surprised and distressed to hear the claim that the Bible condemns astrology, because he was the chief astrologer of Babylon and did exceptionally well, with the help of God.

The only actual mention of astrology in the Old Testament (outside of Daniel) is when the prophet Isaiah warns the Babylonians that God is going to destroy them for their cruelty to the Jews. He tells them that not even astrology will save them (47:13). Any Minister who twists that verse into a condemnation of astrology is truly committing spiritual forgery—taking God's name in vain (blasphemy).

If our modern civilization is doomed to fall, astrology would not be able to save it either. Astrology can only help us to understand the possibilities so we then can take the necessary precautions in order to prevent worst consequences ("to be warned is to be armed").

In the words of Rev. Jacobs, "Astrologers study the rhythm of time, which is the most reliable clock in the world, and Astrology can be conceived as the science of determining the will of God for an individual. The message is in the stars that He placed in the heavens and the laws by which He orders their progress."

These facts are confirmed by the words of Jesus when translated accurately and cleanly from the Greek in which it was originally recorded: "Let your will be done down here on the earth, as perfectly as it appears in the sky." Amen.

Quick Reference

Sagittarius

Aztecs, Spanish Conquest, Marco Polo, China, Roman Catholic Church, Thomas Aquinas, Aristotle, Moslem Migration, Spanish Inquisition, Michelangelo, Raphael, Vatican, Pope Julius II, Martin Luther, Protestant Reformation, European Migrations, American Colonists, American Constitution, Freemasons, Religious Persecutions, Aristotle, Serbia, Kosovo, Balkans, Moslems, Christians, NATO, Ethnic Cleansing, Albanians, India, Pakistan, Armies of God, Evangelicals, Militia, Apocalypse, Oklahoma City, Elections, U.S. Supreme Court, Media, FCC, Palestinians, Israelis, Ethnic Divisions, Terrorism, Patriot Act, Al Qaida, Taliban, Osama Bin Laden, Afghanistan, Iraq, Saudi Arabia, Fundamentalists, Crusade, British, Haiti, Refugees, Biblical Prophecies, Faith-based Initiatives, The Evil Doers, Europeans, Holy Wars, America, Ku Klux Klan, Christian Coalition, Christian Nation, Truth, Zealotry, Infidel, Gandhi, United Nations, U.S. President, Government, Evolution, Creationism, Religious Garments, Passion of The Christ, Gibson, Anti-Semitism, Roman Empire, Pontius Pilate, Jewish High Priests, Blasphemy, Pharisees, Gentiles, Jesus, Gospels, Messiah, Sabath, Easter, Geza Vermes, Constantine, Nicene Creed, Holy Trinity, Angels, Christian Books/Stores/

Clubs, Heavens' Gate Cult, Hale-Bobb Comet, African Sudan, Old Time Religion, NASA, Space, Final Frontier, Columbia, Challenger, Hubble Telescope, Galaxies, Moon Station, Mars Rovers.

Capricorn

Roman Empire, Byzantine Empire, Justinian's Code, Origen, Athens, Second Council Nicaea, Iconoclasm, Veneration, Charlemagne, Church & State, Four Popes Year, Christians, Jews, Clipping Coin, Asen Dynasty, Yuan Dynasty, Teutonic Order, Campanus, New Testament, Luther, Pope Leo X, Explorers, Conquistadors, Caribbean Forts, European Imperialism, Slaves, Commodities, The Prince, Machiavelli, Dominionism, Tyrants, Monarchs, King George, Napoleon, Revolutionary War, U.S. Constitution, Republicans, Social Services, Corporate Empires, Civil Rights, Church/State, Depression, Privatization, Deregulations, Judges, Biblical Laws, National Security, Tax Cuts, National Debt, America's Pluto, Nationalism, Saturn, Unilateralism, Isolationism, Terrorism, American Empire, Forefathers, Freemasons.

Aquarius

Romans, End Persecution, Two Empires, Constantine, Eastern Orthodox, First Council Nicaea, Christ Divinity, Jews, Calendar, Paganism, Turks, Alliances, Treaties, Marco Polo, Spectacles, Byzantines, Ottoman Empire, Constantinople, Spanish Inquisition, Pizarro, Inca of Peru, Brazil, Jesuits Order, Reformation, Pope's Authority, German Bible, Jesus' Jewishness, Unbelievers, Halley's Comet, Copernicus, Solar

System, New Texts, Science, Magnetic Pole, Nostradamus, Predictions, First Maps, Astrology Magazines, Magnetic Pole, French Revolution, Uranus, Group Power, Humanity, Nuclear Weapons, Diversity, World Bank, Genetic Engineering, Electric Vehicles, Technology, Science, Aquarius Age, Vernal Equinox, World Age, Constellations, Jesus' Birth, Age Avatars, Moses, Social Justice.

Pisces

Christian Crusades, Pope Urban II, St. Anselm, Constantine's Sword, Holy Land, War of the Cross, Ritual Murder, Rhineland, Passover, Plagues, Epidemics, Persecutions, Crucifixion, Prophesies, Tobacco, Jesuits, The Zohar, Mysticism, Puritanism, Counter Reformation, Prayer Book, Book of Martyrs, Wars of Religion, Calvinists, Presidential Curse, Jupiter-Saturn, Andrew Jackson, Indian Nation, The Trail of Tears, Pisces Age, Christian Era, Blind Belief, Karma, Enlightenment, New Age, Jesus, Divine Intelligence, Introspection, Inner Peace, Proselytizing, Mantras, Submission, Institutions, Ocean Resources, Petroleum, Pollution, Neptune, World Peace, Know Thy Self, Poison Gases, Redemption, Christian Era, Reincarnation, Self-realization, Astrology, Virgins, Paradise, Heaven, Hell, God's Blessings, Mother Theresa, Divine Justice, Emotional Submission, Awareness.

Aries

Tibet, Buddhism, Prophet Mohammed, Islam, Koran, Arabs in Spain, Hundred Years' War, Spain, Portugal, Gothic Art, Siberia, Ivan IV, Gregorian Calendar, Catacombs, Tycho,

Kepler, Shakespeare, Drake, Queen Elizabeth I, English Colonies, West Indies, Mary Queen of Scots, Japan, Joseph Smith, Mormon Church, Mohammed, Socialism, Independence, Liberty, Dickens, Communist Manifesto, End Inquisition, Neptune, Civil War, New Religion, Visions, Blind-believers, Buddhism, Cosmic Law.

Taurus

Mexico, Aztecs, China's Wall, The Bastille, Gothic Cathedrals, Renaissance, Copper Coins, Manhattan Island, Taj Mahal, USA Postal Service, Civil War, The Union, Abolition, American Values, Origin of the Species, Italy, Industrial Revolution, Buildings, Bridges, Papal Infallibility, Immaculate Conception, KKK, Evangelism, In God We Trust, Future Presidents, Multi-millionaires, Industrialists, Reconstruction, Infrastructure, Financial Markets, Corporate Empires, Dependable Substances.

Gemini

Union of Kalmar, Greek Literature, Chinese Encyclopedia, Bellifortis, Universities, Galileo, Isaac Newton, William Lilly, Universities, Literacy, Scientific Geniuses, Intellectual Explosion, New Inventions, Industrial Revolution, Einstein, Ford's Model T, The Wright Brothers, Walt Disney, Franklin D. Roosevelt, Edgar Casey, Inventions, Education, Transportation, Communication, Exploration, Astrology, Academe, New Age Avatar.

Cancer

Joan of Arc, Double-Eagle, Order of Golden Fleece, Conte du Dauphine, Negroes at Cape Blanc, Homesteads, Native Americans, Africans, Slave Trade, Salem Witch-hunt, Women's Vote, '20s Boom, America's Image & Citizens, Immigrants, Market Crash 1929, Depression, Unions, Ethnic Identities, Pluto's discovery, America's Sun, World Wars, Communist Revolution, British, Iraq, Spain, WWII Women, Women's Issues, Prime Ministers, Patriotism, Nationalism.

Leo

European Renaissance, Golden Age, Byzantine Empire, Imperialism, Divine Rights of Monarchs, Conquerors, Empire of Nicaea, The Franciscans, Fall of Constantinople, Turks killed Emperor Constantine, Pope Innocent III, Jews Banned, Passion Plays, Leonardo Da Vinci, Columbus, Vespucci, The New World, The Gold Rush, Decimation Indian Nations, Dictators, Holocaust, Hitler, Pearl Harbor, McCarthyism, Atomic Bombs, Disneyland, Hollywood, Movie Stars, Big bands, Television, Baby Boomers, Dot/Com Bull Markets, Corporate Empires, Retirement, Social Security, Privileged Few.

Virgo

London Houses, Newgate Prison, Denmark, Vienna, Printing Press, Copenhagen, Reading Bible forbidden, Leprosy, Dante, German Bible, Ferdinand, Isabella, Inquisitors, Heresy, Commerce, Slave Trade, Hospitals, Libraries, Universities, Banks, English Colonies, Spanish Empire, Sputnik,

Moon Landing, Ecology, Cuban Missiles Crises, Berlin Wall, Czechoslovakia, USSR, Cold War, Civil Rights, Kennedy Brothers, Dr. King, Vietnam War, U.S. National Guard, Activists, Labor Unions, World Bank, Trade Organizations, Unions, Armed Forces, Security.

Libra

The Dominicans, Spanish Inquisition, Ferdinand, Queen Isabella, Christopher Columbus, End Moorish Kingdom in Spain, New Cultures, Treaties, Freemasons, Poor Richard's Almanac, European Parliament, Space Agency, Women's Liberation Movement, Sexual Revolution, Disco, Porno, Prime Ministers, Watergate, Peace Summit, Leftist Guerrillas, China, Panama Canal, Shah of Iran, Ajatollah Khomeini, Saddam Hussein, Bahamas, Israel/Arab War, Chile, Argentina, Bahamas, Jonestown Cult, Communes, Manson Family, Swingers, Generation X, Rappers, Mush Pit, Teams, Legal System, Women's and Gay Rights, International Relationships, Middle East.

Scorpio

Arabs took Jerusalem, Moslem Kingdom in Spain, Alhambra Palace, Seventh Crusade, Pinnacle Spanish Inquisition, Instruments of Torture, Burning Books, Heresy, Syphilis Epidemic, Orphanages, Piracy, Machiavelli, New Taxes, Scotland, England's Crown Opposed, Reformation, Intrigue, Power Struggles, Cold War, Evil Empire, Taliban, Afghanistan, Panama, Granada, Iraq, Iran-Contra Scandal, South America, Contra-Narcotic Wars, Drug Lords, CIA, Cuba, Operation Moses, Indira Gandhi, Greed, S & L Banks,

Evangelical Empire, Ferdinand Marcos, Corazon Aquino, Jean-Claude Duvalier, Aids, Rwanda, Somalia, Ethiopia, Bosnia, Marshall Tito, Yugoslavia, Lebanon, Corruption, Genocide, Massacres, Famine, Kuwait, Gulf War, Saddam Hussein, Spies, FBI, End Russian Communism, New Age Movement, Channelers, Ramtha, Faith Healers, Berlin Wall, Dr. Kevorkian, Hurricane Andrew, Insurance Industry, Waco, Koresh, ATF, Catholic Priests, Sex Scandals, Impeachment, Rightwing Conspiracy, Trial of the Century, The Dream Team, Internet, Gothic, Greed is Good, Born Killers, Satanic Cults, Teenage Suicide, Superstitious people, Religious Fanatics, Heaven, Paradise, Hidden Mysteries.

Bibliography

Defining Relationships Astrologically—A Simplified Course in the Symbolic Language of the Art/Science of Astrology, Theresa H. McDevitt, The Venus Press, Jupiter, FL

Tables of Planetary Phenomena. Neil F. Michelsen, Pluto Ingresses, ACS Publications Inc., San Diego, CA

The Timetables of History, The New Third Revised Edition. Simon & Schuster, New York, NY

The Universal Illustrated Encyclopedia. Banner Press, Inc., NY.

The Random House Dictionary. The Unabridged Edition, NY.

The Book of World Horoscopes. Nicolas Campion. Antony Rowe Ltd., Wiltshire, England.

Yahoo Internet Web Sites

Astrology's Pew in Church. Don Jacobs. The Joshua Foundation 1979, San Francisco, CA (out of print).

Larousse Encyclopedia of Astrology. McGraw-Hill Book CO, New York, NY.

Holy Bible. G. M. Lamsa's translation from the Aramaic of the Peshitta, authoritative ancient Bible text. Holman Bible Publishers, Nashville, TN.

Constantine's Sword—The Church and the Jews. James Caroll. Houghton Mifflin CO, Boston, New York.

National Geographic magazine (History of Europe).

Americans United for Separation of Church & State, Washington, DC.

Testimony from a Fellow Astrologer

The educated astrologer exists in a unique position. S/he essentially steps out of time to understand the impact long-range cycles bear upon human affairs (both individual and collective). Most people live within the intellectual confines of a given age. It is not until their descendants study history, that the flaws of their collective thought processes are recognized.

Each epoch has its own blind spots, and yet discernible historical patterns are in evidence to those with eyes to see. The astrologer does not wait for the march of time to confirm or deny ignorance and it's far from blissful reflexes. The astrologer can read the writing on the cosmic wall, and is therefore positioned to guide mankind so that the trespasses of time need not recur.

Unfortunately, modern economics tend to reward the unconscionable. As a partial result, conservative right wing publishing houses have made headway into America's mass thinking process. They continue to rest upon medieval prejudices (such as "devil worship") levied against astrology/astrologers and destroy the credibility of our field of inquiry. The same narrow thinking that led to the execution of heretics (astrologers) and others seeking a truth that transcends the rigid parameters of the patriarchal church-state has returned to our land. It shapes thinking with miss-information.

As Theresa McDevitt points out in this book, the study of Pluto's cycle relates with profound, prophetic detail the legacy of time, and how it imprints the affairs of mankind. The stars do not cause these events; however, given the nature of our holographic universe, they portend them.

Like a stellar map, they show us where we are going. Wrought by Creator into the heavens, the planets were designed to act as navigational aids, just as ancient explorers aimed their sextants to the stars in order to reach uncharted territories.

I salute all those who have found the courage to pursue a wider understanding of their experience by venturing into astrological theory for compelling answers to this vast mystery we term life. Also, I hope you, the reader; gain useful productive insights from Ms. McDevitt's book.

An awareness of higher truth can elucidate minds in a time when the final nebulous din of the Piscean age falls like a great fog over far too many intelligent persons, blinding them to the truth that shall set them free (of Piscean Age illusions and the fish against fish metaphorical, ideological Armageddon it has come down to). May the stars be with you.

Sioux Rose
Author of The Alchemy of Fusion

About the Author

Theresa H. McDevitt is a professional astrologer, certified by the American Federation of Astrologers and Professional Astrologers Inc. She is also a hypnotherapist, certified by the American Council of Examiners. Theresa is an spiritual minister, having been ordained by Mission Aquarius, Inc. and New Age Spiritual Helpers Church. She also holds various degrees in astrology and metaphysics from The Rosicrucian Fellowship and The Mayan Order Society.

Theresa is an experienced astrologer and metaphysician, specializing in relationships and past life therapy. She counsels, teaches and lectures in these subjects. Her articles are published in most major astrological publications and other local and foreign magazines. Theresa is also fluent in the Spanish language.

Defining Relationships Astrologically, written by this author, presents a simplified and original method for teaching and learning the symbolic art/science of astrology. The 16 two-sided, color-coded, cutout cards included in this book offer an exceptional method for easier and faster learning. In addition, the book features the understanding of the composite method for defining all types of relationships: romantic, family, business, and friendship. (A second edition of this book will soon be published.)

Why History Repeats features the precise cyclical and evolutionary process of civilization. This book conveys the message that increased awareness of planetary cycles accelerates the spiral growth process towards world harmony and progress.

Theresa McDevitt's books are designed to facilitate comprehension of the correlation between the mystical and the scientific, thus benefitting the students of metaphysics, as well as the general public.